NEXT TR
TO THE TOWER

by

STEVE PALMER

1st Edition - 1965   2nd Edition - 1997   3rd Edition - 2004

© STEVE PALMER - TRAMROAD HOUSE

AUTHOR'S COMMENTS TODAY

This is the third edition of "NEXT TRAM TO THE TOWER", now completely different to the original book in 1965. That was my first book, and then I said that Blackpool had become Britain's last remaining tramway system, having pioneered the electric street tramways in 1885. Today it is approaching the 120th year of trams on the Promenade, and Britain has now light-rail systems in Manchester, Sheffield, Birmingham, Croydon and Nottingham. Undoubtedly the survival of the trams is because of separate operation on the 1905 Promenade reservation and its connection with the inter-urban Blackpool & Fleetwood Tramroad in 1920. Therefore the trams have become one of the famous attractions of Blackpool, along with the Tower, Pleasure Beach and Illuminations.

In this book you will read about the background to the tramway and its survival, together with some of the characters who have made it famous. Readers will see trams operating in parts of Blackpool where they can no longer run, and trams of many different types, which are recorded in detail. Thus there will be trams, which you no longer can see, and those which have been preserved on museum lines in Britain and U.S.A. To those of you who are interested in the trams, and those of you who enjoy riding on them while being on holiday, I hope that this book will be fascinating – in many ways!

Look Out Trams About!

Steve Palmer March 2004

ACKNOWLEDGEMENTS

I acknowledge all the help and contributions given by: David Helliwell, Editor of THE GAZETTE, Blackpool. Glynn Wilton, Photographic Curator, NATIONAL TRAMWAY MUSEUM, Crich, Derbyshire. PHOTOGRAPHERS: M.J.O'Connor NTM and R.B. Parr NTM.W. R. Buckley, R. P. Fergusson, Bryan Grint, Tony Stevenson, Roy Hubble Collection, A.D.Packer Collection.

Author Steve Palmer framed in the windscreen of Boat 228 at Transbay Terminal, San Francisco in 1986. Our Boat is still flying the Union Jack along with Stars & Stripes.

Contents

Pharos Lighthouse with Pantograph 168.
R. P. Fergusson

Cheers to the future of 761 on 4 June 1979, with Mayor Coun. Bobby Dewhirst,
Transport Chairman Coun. Stan Parkinson, Manager Derek Hyde, and Chief Engineer Stuart Pillar.
The Gazette.

General Managers

John Lancaster	1885 - 1910	25 years
Charles Furness	1910 - 1932	22 years
Walter Luff	1933 - 1954	22 years
J. C. Franklin	1954 - 1974	20 years
D. L. Hyde	1974 - 1986	12 years

Managing Directors

Tony Depledge	1986 - 2001	16 years
Steve Burd	2001 - present	

BLACKPOOL TRAMWAYS ...AT A GLANCE

OPERATOR: Blackpool Transport Services Limited
MANAGING DIRECTOR: Steve Burd
ADDRESS: Transport Offices, Blundell Street, Blackpool
TRAM FLEET: 72 passenger cars, 5 vintage cars,
4 illuminated cars and 4 works cars
SERVICES: Starr Gate & Fleetwood, Starr Gate &
Cleveleys & Promenade
MILEAGE: 11.5 route miles
(6.5 miles of street routes abandoned 1961-3)
GAUGE: 4ft. 8½ ins
LINE VOLTAGE: 550 volts d.c.

Dates to Remember

29 September 1885	Official opening of the conduit tramway system
11 July 1898	First electric car of Blackpool & Fleetwood Tramroad company runs.
7 August 1897	Conduit track laid along Lytham & Station Roads
13 June 1899	Overhead line system adopted in Blackpool
20 May 1901	Trial run on the new Marton Route
13 June 1902	Talbot Square & Layton new route opened
1 January 1920	Blackpool Corporation took possession of the Blackpool & Fleetwood Tramroad
October 1926	Tramway reservation extended – New South Promenade
1 April 1933	Five Year Plan began: modernised fleet, layout, depots
19 October 1936	Conversion of Layton & Central Drive routes to bus operation took place
December 1946	First resilient-wheel PCC-type car 303 was on trial
5 June 1952	First post-war car – Coronation 304 delivered
9 April 1958	Inaugural run of trailer-car set 276 & 275 to Fleetwood
Easter 1958	Double-deck trams ran to Fleetwood for the first time
16 June 1960	New trailer car Tl delivered to Rigby Road Depot
29 September 1960	Jubilee celebrations of the tramway by processions
29 October 1961	Closure of Squires Gate route and track in Station Road and Squires Gate Lane
28 October 1962	Closure of the Marton route and Marton Depot
27 October 1963	Closure of Dickson Road track from Gynn Square to North Station and Bispham Depot
29 September 1985	Centenary of Promenade Tramway – 20 car procession with 6 trams from other systems and steam-tram engine
1 July 1998	Commemoration of first tram to Fleetwood by B & F car 2
12 July 1998	Centenary Day – grand procession of 14 trams from Pleasure Beach to Fleetwood in rain and gale!
23 October 2000	Return of Standard 147 to Blackpool from U.S.A.

In 2000 Engineering car 754 is seen with men working on the overhead bracket-arm in Fleetwood.
Author

Electrical Details

The system is supplied from the National Grid and rectified to 550 volts d.c., originally by five mercury arc rectifiers situated at Bond Street S.S., Gynn Square, Bispham Depot, Thornton Gate and Copse Road Depot Fleetwood. The electrical department of Blackpool Transport looked after the overhead line – running repairs and rewiring. The overhead hangs at nineteen feet above street level and most cars collect current through pantographs, while others have trolley poles with fixed heads and 6 in. wheels. Section-feeders and breakers are indicated by orange diamonds mounted on the poles with them.

In 1995-6 the system was rewired and restructured with new poles – painted maroon and cream – with stainless steel bracket-arms, from Starr Gate to Thornton Gate. New substations were constructed at Pleasure Beach, St. Chads Road, Metropole, Gynn Square and Little Bispham, while those at Kirby Road (in Depot) Bispham and Thornton Gate have been refurbished. North of Thornton Gate the overhead structures and feeders are due for replacement, together with the original substation at former Copse Road depot.

Car Stops & Signs

TRAM STOP: Originally, Request and Compulsory Stops were shown by circular polo-shaped signs and painted green. Today the EEC stop sign is used with the shape of a tram, script in "Tram Stop, Place-name, Northbound or Southbound", and at each stop the timetable is shown.
FACING POINTS: Black dividing lines on white board capped by red triangle.
AT CURVES: At curves and road crossings, poles are fitted with white diamonds showing speed in black numbers before and "END" after. In Cleveleys a speed is "12 Orion Curve" and diamond with vertical line is "signals 50m".
TRAM PINCHES: Dept. of Transport road signs at Metropole & Fleetwood.
TRAM CROSSING: Notices vary from "TRAM CROSSING – BEWARE" & "BEWARE OF THE CARS", to Department of Transport light rail sign.

Track - Permanent Way

The standard railway gauge of 4ft 8½in is used for the system with 109.7lb per yard B.S. Section 8 grooved rail used for street track, paved reservation on the Promenade and road crossings on reservations. Tramroad reservation comprise 85lb bullhead rail – now 95lb – chaired to wooden sleepers. In winters 2002 to 2004 sections of reservation have been relaid by Birse Company, who have used flat-bottom rail held by spring clips and rubber inserts on concrete sleepers. However bullhead rail with double chairs for check rail and wooden sleepers have been used on curves. This new rail at Norbreck to Little Bispham and Thornton Gate to Ash Street, Fleetwood now give a much better tram ride!

Contractors laying the new flat-bottom rail on concrete sleepers, at Rossall Beach in February 2003. *Author*

This is a splendid scene on Central Promenade in the 19th Century, with crowds, conduit car 6, landaus and the new Tower with lift and spiral staircase. Advertising "WINTER GARDENS", 3 - 6 were built at Lancaster Railway Carriage Works. A ride on the open-top deck was a novelty.

                                                        Author's Collection

1885 When it all began

Tuesday, 29th September 1885 proved to be a fete day for Blackpool with the official opening of the new tramway as part of the Lifeboat Fete. Civic dignitaries from all parts of Lancashire gathered to witness a double event. The town was in a holiday mood; large streamers floated from the lamp standards and shopkeepers had decorated their shop frontages. The inauguration of the first street electric tramway was said to "possess elements of unique interest" and "gives Blackpool its own place as a pioneer". The local newspaper, while admitting that electric traction had already been tried elsewhere, dismissed these early trials in contemptuous vein.

"Other towns have the lead in adopting electricity as a motive power for tramway use but in the case of Brighton the electric tramway is little more than a toy and the line running in the North of Ireland is of a type entirely different".

So much for Volks and the Giant's Causeway Tramway, but an element of truth existed under this bombastic extravagance. Undoubtedly Holroyd Smith's system introduced the electric tramway car to the streets of Britain and made urban mass transportation possible for the first time. It remains to the eternal credit of Blackpool that the invention was looked upon, not with suspicion, but as "one of the fairy tales of science". And so to the great day and an eyewitness account:

"Handsome in design and elegant in every detail of its construction, the car was brought up immediately opposite the lifeboat launching ground, here 5 came and there it went palpably without assistance showing the magic of adapted human knowledge. The crowd in the neighbourhood of the car and on the pier was simply astounding. Mr. Holroyd Smith had the honour to demonstrate the utility of electricity as a motive power for tramway propulsion – an invention which yet may revolutionise the vehicular traffic of the world".

Prophetic words indeed and Michael Holroyd Smith was conscious of the significance of his invention when he presented Alderman Harwood, the Mayor of Manchester and opener of the line with an ebony and brass handle upon which was inscribed: "Presented to Alderman Harwood, Mayor of Manchester, by Mr. Holroyd Smith, engineer on the occasion of His Worship inaugurating the Blackpool Electric Tramway, September 29th 1885". The handle was made by Smith Baker & Company of Manchester, the firm that had made the controllers for the ten cars. Thus the new tramway and the lifeboat, Samuel Fletcher, were well and truly launched and Blackpool was again a pioneer!

A century later, on 29th September 1985, the original ebony and brass handle was produced by the Harwood family and used to drive conduit car 4 at the head of a Centenary procession of twenty cars.

In September 1886 Holroyd Smith read a paper before the British Association at Birmingham in which he described his Blackpool tramway system. Some of the early difficulties emerge from his talk and the discussion which followed and some interesting figures for operation are given. The number of passengers carried during a six-day week in the winter of 1885 was 2,393 at a cost of fuel and wages of under £24. In contrast, during the week ending September 4th, 1886, which was the height of the season, the number of passengers carried was 44,306, while the cost of wages and fuel was £45. The figures show that while the number of passengers increased twenty two times the winter figure, the costs less than doubled and demonstrated the unique advantage of the tramway for the first time. However, the promenade line had many disadvantages which are here described by its inventor:

"The Blackpool line is nearly two miles in length. It is a single track with ten passing loops and one single length of double line along central promenade. The engine house and car sheds are placed near the centre and this position was selected as being the most convenient and so offering considerable advantages from an electric point of view. The roadway runs along the sea coast facing directly west and exposed to the full force of the wind and tide from the Irish Sea. So strong are the periodic storms that, though the road level is well above the ordinary high-water mark, the waves wash over in such volumes that the road is flooded and the doors and windows of houses are occasionally beaten in. The difficulties in supplying electricity underground through the conduit in such a situation are therefore unusually great. When the tide is over the line the current of course makes earth. At one time it was intended to employ accumulators for haulage during the flooding and horses were occasionally used, but owing to the amounts of shingle brought over, the grooves in the rails were filled, and the cars kept derailing. Working during the floodings has therefore been abandoned".

Conduit car 4 - a survivor today - showing the bowler-hatted driver holding the hand brake, and the control lever protruding through the stairway. The top-deck passengers are sitting back-to-back, and their car has just passed Robert's Oyster Bar.   *Roy Hubble Collection.*

A scene in 1899, with ex-conduit car 3 fited with a twenty-foot trolley pole reaching out to the new side-overhead. Car 3 is heading for Victoria Pier via Lytham Road and is well-filled, but not the horsedrawn bus - soon to be banned from the Promenade.
W. R. Buckley.

The generators, situated behind the depot in Blundell Street, could produce a maximum force of 300 volts, but trouble was experienced with conductivity – the actual resistance being more than calculated. Holroyd Smith gave some interesting figures, which show the fall in voltage over the line:

"At the tram shed, where the current was fed direct to the conduit contactors, there was an electromotive force of 230 volts and at Foxhall – the junction with the main line – 210 volts. At the north end of the line, Cocker Street, it was reduced to 185 volts and at the south end of the line, Victoria Pier – 168 volts".

He attributed this fall in voltage to poor joints and faulty connections and pointed out that after a night of heavy rain or sea flood there was a serious loss of conductivity. The efficiency of the generator was 90%, whereas that of the cars was only 45% and thus more perfect insulation needed to be achieved.

In 1892 the Corporation took over from the Electric Tramway Company, switched the supply to its own power station and extended the conduit line along Station Road in 1897, linking Lytham Road track with the Promenade at Victoria Pier. However, after continuing problems in 1899 the overhead line was erected and the Board of Trade inspected it on 13th June. When it came into use on the 21st the conduit was still live and could be used by cars having problems in losing their trolleys, until all was satisfactory. This was caused by the 20-foot trolley poles, working at right angles to the overhead mounted on short bracket-arms. The opening of the new Blackpool & Fleetwood Tramroad in 1898 gave a successful example of the light rail system with the overhead line. The original conduit system provided undoubted problems for trams on a seashore tramway. However, it has to be pointed out that the London trams successfully operated on a large conduit system until its closure in 1952.

1898 The New Tramroad

The construction of the Blackpool & Fleetwood Tramroad commenced in 1897 by the Company which could see the importance of linking the popular resort of Blackpool with the important seaport of Fleetwood. The construction of the line crossed the "bleak and rugged cliffs of Bispham and the desolate stretch of Norbreck", intending that it would open up the coast for the visitors to Blackpool. This was a light railway with fixed stopping places over the 8.5 miles with street tramways at each end. Blackpool refused to allow the company to construct its line along the sea front having acquired Claremont Park in 1896, and thus the line was directed along the back road to Talbot Road Station. From King Edward Avenue to the station the Borough built the line and leased it to the company for 21 years. In Fleetwood the company constructed the line with the option of the U.D.C. able to buy it after 30 years. "The Experimental Opening – An Exhilarating Ride" came on 1st July 1898, when Crossbench car 4 took a party of Blackpool Council, Transport Department and the press for the first ride to Fleetwood. "A large number of people crowded the street in front of the Talbot Road Station and gave a hearty send off to the party at 3.10pm". As "Father of Blackpool", Ald. Cocker said "You cannot have smooth sailing on the first trial", since the street track was full of grit. Once outside the town boundary the ride improved over the sleeper track and a passenger said "The feeling was grand". When the tram arrived at Fleetwood Ash Street, a large crowd had gathered and children from a local school cheered to welcome it. Car 4 was parked in West Street while the party went for lunch and the return journey also paused at Cleveleys Hotel, where Ald. Cocker proposed a toast to the company's success!

Blackpool & Fleetwood Tramroad 4 - the first tram in Fleetwood - parked outside the famous Lofthouse's Chemist and surrounded by curious locals and the crew.   *Author's Collection.*

An early scene of crossbench car 5 in Dickson Road, with two crews, an inspector and electrician posed in front of it. We know John Lingard who is wearing an overcoat and a driver's badge. Notice the striped blinds held up by straps, a trailer connection-socket and the adverts for EAT HOVIS BREAD and ROUNTREE'S COCOA on seats and running-board.
Audrey Bendall

The Board of Trade inspection took place on 13th July and there were protests by bus owners that Warbreck Road was too narrow, and thus trams first operated from Gynn Square the next day, until the road was widened by 29th September. The inspectors visited Bispham Depot and the generating power station, first travelling down the cutting from Bispham Top. A tram depot and yard was also built in Copse Road Fleetwood, where there was a link with the railway line, thus able to bring coal to Bispham. Also there was a small depot at the Bold Street terminus, for the first and last cars each day. From 14th July the line opened and for the first twelve months almost one million and a half passengers were carried over the system! Undoubtedly the commercial development of the Tramroad was seen in publicity as: "One of the Joys of Life" and "Don't Miss Your Invigorating Ride to Blackpool". Of course the link with the daily sailing of the Isle of Man boat from Fleetwood also attracted riders on the trams. At the beginning, connection with the company cars at Gynn Square was provided by landaus from the town centre. In 1900 Blackpool Borough built their own line to Gynn Square, through the recently acquired Claremont Park. While Blackpool used open-top cars – like the unique Dreadnoughts – the Tramroad Company operated single-deck cars of two types – crossbench open-sided and saloon cars – each suitable for the weather. John Cameron, the manager, rode round the system once a day, ensuring efficient operation by 80 staff.

1920 – AMALGAMATION OF TRAMROAD & TRAMWAY

Since the Blackpool & Fleetwood Tramroad Company had been successful, commercial development took place along the coastal line. However, the future of the Company was questioned when Bispham UDC became part of Blackpool in 1917 and the lease on its track in the Borough would end in 1919. Therefore, negotiations secretly took place between the Mayor Ald. Lindsey Parkinson and company manager John Cameron. When Lancashire & Yorkshire Railway also became interested in purchasing the Tramroad Company Blackpool Borough increased its offer to £284,000. This succeeded in securing its possession of the Tramroad on 1st January 1920. The amalgamation thus ensured the link between the Promenade tramway and the coastal line to Fleetwood. This enlarged Blackpool's fleet from 84 to 125 trams and the company trams were renumbered 101-141. The first task was to physically join the tracks, with curves, to the Promenade line at Gynn Square and to Talbot Road line on the Layton route. While the ex-company cars continued to operate the traditional route to Fleetwood, Promenade open-top trams would start operating to Bispham, once North Promenade reservation and Gynn Square layout took place in 1924. Blackpool Transport modernised the Fleetwood lines by re-aligning the Rossall track away from the front of Rossall School to facilitate the construction of Broadway. In May 1925 a loop-line was built to the Fleetwood Ferry terminus, with the trams passing the Pharos Lighthouse. Also the centre poles in Lord Street were removed and replaced by span-wires suspended from side poles. A special tram was now operated each day from North Pier at 9-45 to connect with the Isle of Man steamer from Fleetwood. Also the Goods & Mineral Service ran along the tramway from the railway at Copse Road to Thornton Gate sidings, thus linking Thornton Station with Cleveleys. All this sought to ensure a successful future for the enlarged Municipal Tramway system.

Fleetwood Lord Street in 1926 with the new span-wires, and renumbered car 134 about to pass Tilling Stevens bus on route 11. The J. W. Fish shop is still there today!   *Author's Collection*

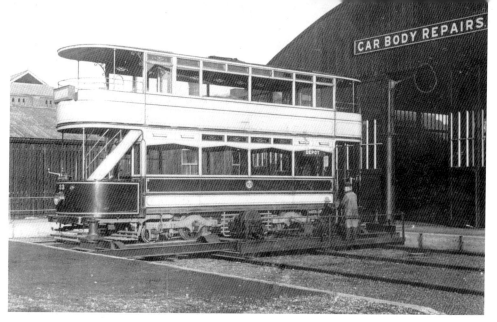

New Standard 33 in front of the Car Body Repair Shop on the traverser, about to be moved sideways to join the running-fleet in Blundell Street depot.   *Author's Collection.*

The Twenties in Blackpool was a momentous time for the Tramway and the revival of the illuminations in 1925. The opening of new works at Rigby Road was created from four old aircraft hangars, thus enabling the Transport Department to maintain the fleet, including rebuilding five ex-company "Yanks" as "Glasshouses". More importantly, they also built 35 new Standard cars and 6 Toastracks between 1924 & 1927. Apart from these achievements, it should be added that two new illuminated trams were built: in 1926 the Lifeboat from Marton box-car 40 for the Municipal Jubilee, and in 1927 the elegant Gondola from 28. These became a trio with De-Luxe car 78 which was first created in 1912 to celebrate the opening of Princess Parade. The other new trams included seven Standards 146-152 built by Hurst Nelson and ten new "Pullman" cars 167-176 built by E. E. Dick Kerr in 1928. These handsome saloon cars were fitted with pantographs and were destined to operate a 12-minute service on the North Station & Fleetwood route, ironically lasting until 1961! They were first towed to Bispham Depot, since the Promenade tramway overhead was supported by rigid bracket-arms. A steeple-cab electric locomotive was acquired from English Electric in 1928, for towing the railway wagons to Thornton Gate sidings. It is interesting that the final Standard tram 177 was built in 1929, from all the remaining suitable fittings and timber in the works. During this decade there was a full programme of track-relaying, including doubling the street-track to North Station and making a reserved-track tramway along North Promenade by the creation of a cantilever footpath over the Middle Walk. New South Promenade with a tramway extension to Starr Gate was completed in October 1926. Thus the Circular Tours were extended round Squires Gate Lane and the Fleetwood service became eleven and a half miles long!

1932 Vintage Tramway Year

During the significant period of development of the Tramway, 1932 marks the end of an era before modernisation begins. Charles Furness made his last report to the Transport Committee as General Manager declaring a gross profit of £92,045 for 1931, while the cars ran a total of 3,472,302 miles – over 39.6 track miles! By this year 167 trams were in stock, including 46 new cars and 62 buses. While receipts appear to be good Mr. Furness sounded a chill note in his report: "The past year has been one of some anxiety, the increasing competition of motor coaches diverting visitors from our pleasure services and the Circular Tours, is shown in the reduced earning per car mile on the Promenade: from 30s.26d in 1929 to 27s.05d in 1931. Whilst the Circular Tour has maintained a good average of 51s.57d per car mile the total receipts have fallen considerably during the past five years". The fall in passenger receipts may not have been entirely due to competition since unemployment was rising. In those days to have a regular job on the tramways was to possess a reasonable amount of security. Motormen were paid a weekly wage of £2.18.0d and guards slightly less. A veteran of those days recalls the rigid discipline of being in municipal uniform: "For running with your front step down you were given two days suspension. There was no brewing on the road but your wife was allowed to bring your tea or lunch to you at the terminus". Blackpool was a busy system of junctions, passing-loops and single tracks. The illuminations period of 31 days extended the season and brought a great deal of useful revenue for the Transport Department. The manager reported: "The volume of traffic during the busy evenings on many occasions reached a figure of 80 cars per hour passing certain points on the Promenade and from Pleasure Beach to Talbot Square, 100 cars per hour". 1932 was described as "wet and stormy", however, the tramway barometer indicated "change" ahead. So much was to be changed in the years ahead, let us therefore remember 1932 as a vintage year of Blackpool Tramways.

Toastrack 81 in Talbot Square 1931, with its crew waiting to start the Circular Tour. Standard 100 is now fully enclosed (see opposite) and bound for Victoria Pier.   *M. J. O'Connor NTM*

Great Storms for the Trams!

A fascinated crowd watch 28 on its side, after the top deck has been removed. Standard 100 may tow the bottom-deck of 28 back to the depot, once upright!   The Gazette.

The coastal tramway has always been hectic for trams, especially when a hurricane occurs. The great storm of 28-29th October 1927 was one of the worst that the Fylde Coast ever experienced. Winds were blowing up to 90mph, sea defences were broken at Fleetwood, and a torrent of sea-water swept through the town. The tram track between Rossall and Fleetwood was submerged, and the ballast washed away. At Blackpool the tram service continued, and the wind created the worst effect the goggled tram drivers on unvesibuled trams fought their way through the hurricane, but one tram did not make it. Standard 28 – one of the latest type – left Bispham for the Pleasure Beach at 10-45 p.m. and was blown over at Richmond Place, before reaching the Cabin. Fortunately there were no passengers, and the crew escaped injury although 28 had toppled over. While laying on its side it had brought down the railings. Though 28 was only a few weeks old, its upper and lower decks were taken to the Works and re-assembled once again!

Subsequently during the Second World War on 6th December 1940, Standard 50 was overturned as caught by a gust of gale-force wind, while it emerged from behind the Metropole Hotel. Like in the case of 28, Standard 50 was split into halves, then loaded by RAF troops and taken back to Rigby Road. All sections of the Standard 50 were in the depot yard by 7p.m. and a tram which had left that morning in one piece, arrived back in three large pieces!

So next time you are on a Standard 147 during a gale, remember the days that 28 and 50 overturned, and hold tight!

1933 – A SENSATION OF STREAMLINERS

The first streamlined car 200, seen on test in the seeming rural grounds of the English Electric Works, Strand Road, Preston, before leaving for Blackpool.   *Official E.E.*

The year 1933 saw changes to the tramway with the appointment of a new General Manager, Walter Luff. Looking around he came to the conclusion that he had inherited a very mixed bag of a fleet with veteran Dreadnoughts 15 & 16 of 1898 and ex company crossbench cars of the same vintage. With the prospective competition of the Ribble Bus Company and motor coaches affecting revenue from the Circular Tour, Walter Luff reported to the Transport Committee about a new type of tramcar with a streamlined appearance, by English Electric of Preston. They had produced many trams before but had not designed a rail coach with an unusual centre entrance and comfortable seating in each saloon. The Transport Committee were so impressed by the design of the new tramcar that they allowed Walter Luff to order one.

Number 200 arrived on 19 June in the new fleet livery of green and cream and went on display at the Gynn Square siding for the interest of delegates to the Municipal Transport Managers' Conference. Complete with a pantograph it offered free demonstration runs for the delegates, met with general acclaim and this resulted in an order for twenty-four more rail coaches like 200. Since these were to be used particularly on the Blackpool & Fleetwood service its design was important to provide passengers with good observation and thus had curved glass windows lining the edge of the roof. This facility would also be particularly useful during the illuminations, when passengers would be able to look up at the features.

The car was quite unlike anything which had appeared before with clear design lines culminating in a rounded front which tapered suddenly into a centre line. Other unusual distinctive features included twin indicators, windscreens and headlamps. The passengers entered at the centre on a low platform and had the choice of the two saloons which were equipped with reversible moquette seats, clocks and floor heaters. Ventilation was all-important and in addition to four half-drop windows in each saloon, the roofs could be opened by a long sliding panel. This could be done by the conductor using a handle to wind it back and it became known as the "sunshine roof". Thus the rail coach could be made into a semi-open tram according to the weather!

The new cars were a sensation when they first appeared on the Promenade and the passengers waved passed old trams in order to ride on the rail coaches. Upon entrance to the centre platform they would remove their hats and look for the doormats to wipe their feet – like home. Certainly this had been a sensation and improved the image of the Blackpool trams in the Thirties. To the tram drivers, who had stood for many hours in the wind and rain swathed in oilskins on the open platforms of the old cars this new railcoach with enclosed cabs and driver's seats must have seemed like a "Seventh Heaven"!

The foundation was being laid in August 1933 for a new fleet and the days of the unique Dreadnoughts – which Walter Luff had described as "monstrosities" – were numbered. The Transport Committee were told that a number of trams were unsuitable for summer traffic and showed them drawings of a new 92-seat open-topper and a modern open single-decker. The latter would improve on the Toastracks, without the objections of a clinging conductor and steps over the wheels. Mr. Luff reported an offer by English Electric Company to build one of each type of tramcar to the end of 1933 and quoted a price for an additional twenty-five of each kind before the beginning of the 1934 season. Clearly the English Electric Company had made its terms competitive in the need for a bulk order from Blackpool. Cautious as always, the Committee accepted the offer of the two sample types and left any further decision until they had seen them.

A passenger boards 200 at Gynn Square in 1933, contrasting with the Lytham St. Annes Pullman car which reverses here. A railcoach thus can provide better journeys.   M. J. O'Connor NTM

Walter Luff's Five Year Plan

In January 1934 Mr. Luff was able to report to his Committee that the two experimental cars would be ready for inspection Standing on the street siding in Talbot Square, they made an impressive pair: a large modern open-top car and a boat-like single decker with a canopy over its centre platform. The local press was enthusiastic in its reaction. "There was a rush to see the new Blackpool trams in Talbot Square today, the first two examples of the new types were open for public inspection..... and they wholeheartedly expressed their praise". Once again the power of propaganda helped Mr. Luff to achieve his aim, for the Transport Committee authorised orders to be placed with the E.E. Company for eleven more open "Boats", 12 modern open-toppers and 14 fully-enclosed double-deckers with luxury railcoach features. Of course this began Walter Luff's Five Year Plan, which by 1939 had accomplished the greatest achievement for Blackpool Transport!

In 1934, the second year of the "Five Year Plan" saw the delivery of the twelve open-toppers, which with 226 were numbered 237-249. These were unique in the annals of the British tramway history, in that they represented the only "second generation" of open-toppers. Although primarily designed for summer use the design allowed the upper deck to be closed off by pulling down steel shutter blinds on each of the two staircases. On the top deck were wooden reversible seats, the passengers being protected by the side panelling surmounted by stainless steel handrails. 54 passengers could thus be seated on the top deck, while the two lower saloons could seat 40. With a total of 94 seats the new cars surpassed the capacity of the Dreadnoughts they were intended to replace. The new open-toppers weighed 22 tons, thus having bogies of longer wheelbase, and Z6 controller with a field-shunt notch allowing them to run at 31 m.p.h. on the reservation. The lower saloons were similar to the railcoaches with reversible moquette seating, half-drop windows but a grab rail in the ceiling. The profile of the twelve new open-toppers was slightly more sloped than the upright appearance of 237.

Seen from the Clifton Hotel in Talbot Square, Boat 235 is waiting for customers on the Circular Tour, while another Boat car approaches on the Promenade.   *G. L. Gundry*

A famous scene of the new streamliners, lined-up outside Blundell Street depot on 20 May 1934: open-top 226, Boat 225 and Railcoach 205. *Author's Collection*

The open "boat" car 225 was intended to give all the best features of the traditional "toastrack" cars, while incorporating the safety of the centre loading platform, side panels and a centre gangway. The other eleven "boat" cars 226-236 were delivered during 1934 and had sides level with the seat tops, thus higher than 225. Thus the staff called 225 "Little Willy"! At first the "boats" operated alongside their toastrack predecessors, which were finally withdrawn at the end of the Thirties. By the Easter of 1934 twenty-five trams of the vintage B & F type: "Glasshouses" & "Box-cars" were replaced by the 24 streamlined railcoaches. These first went into service on the North Station & Cleveleys route and then took over the North Station & Fleetwood service. The production railcoaches were different from 200 in several ways, being 3 feet longer with more room for the driver and between the seats. In the cab of 200 it had been difficult for the driver to sit down because the cab was so narrow and thus was not comfortable. The new streamlined trams became very popular in Blackpool as they replaced older trams with high steps and draughts inside.

By 15 December 1934 the first of the enclosed double-deckers – 250 –went into service on the Squires Gate route replacing the traditional Standards then only ten years old. Subsequently it was found that the "Balloons", which they were named, remained in service on this route until it closed in 1961. At the end of the 1934 season twenty Dreadnoughts were taken to Fleetwood Copse Road depot where they were scrapped. At the eleventh hour a telephone call from Walter Luff, the General Manager, gave the workers instructions to save 59. In the Evening Gazette a valedictory tribute said: "They were clumsy, awkward and dangerous but they were Blackpool's own unique trams." I think it would have been nice to announce the passing of these old trams". The retention of 59 was announced and the Evening Gazette responded: "Sometime in the future it may be possible to resurrect the old car and parade it on the Promenade". Well it did happen in 1960 for the 75th anniversary of the Blackpool Tramway and again in 1985 for the Centenary of the Tramway.

With a fleet of 64 streamlined cars secured, including the double-deck cars 250-263, Walter Luff continued to press for a new depot at Rigby Road. The Borough Surveyor had prepared plans in February and tenders were accepted for pile driving, steelwork, brick-work and the track layout. The latter was being undertaken by Edgar Allen Company of Sheffield. Once construction had begun it was proposed that the bus garage should be extended to the same depth as the tram depot. This was designed to cater for the growing bus fleet which was to include buses with centre entrances in line with the current tramcar practice here. The new depot opened on 7 June 1935 taking over operation of the Fleetwood route from Bispham depot, which was reduced in status from a full-scale running depot to a store for the remaining B & F Tramroad cars and the toastracks. With increased depot accommodation plentiful the new depot could take more than 108 cars on 18 tracks. In 1936 twenty of the second series of the English Electric rail coaches 264-283 were delivered before the season. They replaced the remaining Box cars with their corner entrances and high steps which were inadequate for frequent stops and rapid loading.

It is interesting to mention that Lytham St. Annes blue cars were still operating into Blackpool as far as Gynn Square but as compared with the new streamlined fleet looked very outdated. Negotiations for its purchase by Blackpool were very protracted since Walter Luff was keen to operate trams along the whole Fylde Coast. However, since Lytham St. Annes did not want such operation in its territory there was a final attempt for Blackpool to extend the Promenade tramway reservation to St. Annes Square. Sadly, because of the casting vote of Lytham St. Annes' Mayor, the proposal was rejected and a fine prospect for St. Annes & Fleetwood by tram was lost for ever. However, at the end of the season Blackpool trams operated finally on the street routes to Layton and Central Station via Central Drive. This was part of the Five-Year Plan to remove trams, since each route contained single track running along congested streets in the town centre. Conversion to bus operation would transfer the profit from these busy lines from tram to bus balance sheets. The trams were replaced by bus services 22 and 23 operating from Layton to Marton Depot via Talbot Road, Promenade, Central Drive and Waterloo Road. All cars on the Marton route then operated to Royal Oak, and South Pier in the summer season.

Pleasure Beach terminus in 1936 provides a nostalgic sight of the Lytham St. Annes open-topper 40 bound for St. Annes Square, and the new Blackpool railcoaches.   *A. D. Packer Collection.*

An interesting scene at Gynn Square in 1934, showing five generations of the Blackpool fleet: Box-car and Pantograph-car on route 1, Dreadnought, Railcoach and Standard together with Lytham St. Annes Pullman car on the Promenade route.

Since the Pantograph cars were only bought in 1928 for the Fleetwood line, it was important to retain and modernise them in 1936-7. They would appear in a cream livery with only the roof in green and the fleet number would be carried in numerals above the centre saloon pillar. The original trolley tower was shorted by 15 inches from its tall height designed for pantographs, platform folding doors were fitted and new chromium-plated windscreen frames with air-operated wipers were an improvement. Inside the saloons all woodwork was grained and varnished and the ceiling panels painted in white enamel. Finally, a new curved indicator box was made for each end of the roof, replacing the former angular type. Thus they looked very smart and most of these ten cars appeared like this by 1937, still on the North Station & Fleetwood service. In following the progress of the Pantograph cars we must not allow the other events of 1936 to pass us by. The bus fleet was augmented by 25 double-deckers for the tram-conversion built by Leyland and Burlingham. In September Walter Luff was authorised to advertise for tenders to supply a further 20 single-deck cars. For the first time since the plan began the contracts were awarded to the Brush Company of Loughborough to make the bodies, E.M.B. to supply the bogies and Crompton Parkinson & Allen West for the traction equipment.

1937 – Proved to be an Interesting Year

Walter Luff had new development schemes, starting with the opening of the double-track loop at the Pleasure Beach in August, which facilitated the turning of many trams at this famous location. He also had an interesting plan to divert the tramlines from the street at the side of the Metropole Hotel and locate them on the west side. The idea was accepted in principle but not acted upon because of the location of the War Memorial. Since the Lytham St. Annes tramway was due to close on 27 April it was proposed for Blackpool to acquire the track in Squires Gate Lane and Clifton Drive and thus facilitate the continuation of Circular Tours. "Journey's End For Blue Cars" came on 28 April with a special run by 41 from St. Annes Square to the depot in Squires Gate Lane for members of the Council. This last car, built in 1924 by English Electric, was an unvestibuled double-deck car mounted on a four-wheel P22 truck and was retained in the depot only to be subsequently broken-up for the War effort. Following the closure of this tramway Blackpool operated joint bus routes 11 and 11A to Lytham St. Annes from Central Station. Since this was the fourth year of the plan a new three-storey Transport Office was built in Rigby Road and can be seen to this day in the art deco style. Extension to the works was made at this time which today includes the body, painting and fitting shops. Walter Luff proposed further turning loops at Little Bispham and Starr Gate. Construction started and they were opened in 1938. Plans were in hand for the complete relaying of the Lytham Road track and the Station Road branch line which would cost £45,075.

Assembly of the new Brush railcars in The Loughborough Works, showing the wooden frame of one and panelling the shape of the others in a new streamlined style. *NTM Collection.*

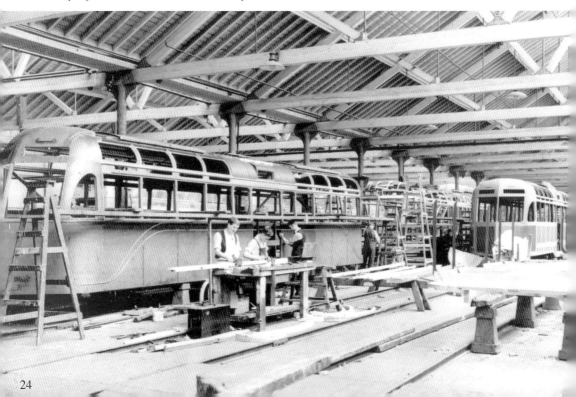

Seen at Rossall in 1937, the Brush railcar is shown in its original livery style, with its front sliding roof open and stainless steel gleaming. This is how 298 should look when restored by Keith Terry.   *Author's Collection.*

The 20 new Brush cars 284-303 were delivered during the summer months. Although they had the same layout as the 45 E.E. railcoaches they were quite distinctive in appearance and called railcars. The fronts were sharply tapered and an innovation was the air-operated sliding platform doors, which could be operated by conductor or driver. All the saloon windows were of the full-drop winding type while the sunshine sliding roof had much longer opening panels sliding underneath the trolley gantry. In the saloons there were heaters at floor-level, clocks over the cab doors and saloon lighting from glazed panels above the windows, seen outside by green glass panels. The ceilings were completed by Alhambrinal panelling, lined in two shades of brown. The bodies were mounted on E.M.B. bogies, familiar on many other systems but seen for the first time in Blackpool. Since they were of the lightweight type the flexible axle bogies were a considerable improvement over the E.E. type and gave much better riding qualities. The Brush cars could always be distinguished by the chrome flares on each side and the second ten had the "V" shape at each end. They operated at first from the new depot on a Squires Gate & Fleetwood route. It is true that the automatic doors were once operated by the driver on the off-side, thus allowing a load of suitcases fall into Lytham Road in the path of a following bus. While thirteen Brush cars still operate today, during 1940-1963 they did operate on the North Station & Fleetwood route from Bispham Depot. For the 1937 illuminations it was decided to replace the De-luxe car 68 by a modern illuminated car. It was designed in streamlined style, its profile lined in coloured lights with opaque windows illuminated from inside showing the shadows of passengers. However, it was built upon the oldest B & F car 141.

Blackpool – A System To Be Proud Of

With 1938 came the final year of the Five Year Plan during which the new turning loops at Starr Gate and Little Bispham were complete in May and June respectively. The discussion of the Metropole street track was still in the news and to counter the objections of the hotel Walter Luff came up with a scheme to include the existing track on a paved reservation which narrowed the pavements and therefore nothing materialised. In October it was proposed to run buses on Lytham Road while the tram track was being renewed. After the outcry which followed the tramway abandonments of 1936 it was decided to relay the Marton route once the work on Lytham Road was completed. It was proposed that a single track would be laid in the centre of Talbot Road along Abingdon Street and down Clifton Street, thus making a one-way system. Fifteen double-deck cars were to be purchased for the Marton route and plans were designed by English Electric. These would be a shorter version of the 1934 Balloons which would have three-window saloons and 72 seats. When the Second World War broke out in September 1939 none of these developments took place and it was a sense of "make do and mend". However, a modern, streamlined fleet had been created to match all of the old types bar one and that was the semi-open B & F crossbench cars. In November 1938 a design for its modern equivalent was designed by English Electric. Twelve of these sun-saloons would be built, having wooden reversible seats, half-open windows and a centre folding canvas roof but they would use equipment from older cars. They were not delivered until the outbreak of war, numbered 10-21 and ironically did become troop-carriers and had to be enclosed! (see Car Types for details).

Constrasting styles of double-deckers at North Pier in June 1940, with masked and hooded headlamps for the War. There is still a chance of riding on an open-topper!   *M. J. O'Connor*

The delightful Gondola, taking official passengers round the Illuminations, including General Manager Walter Luff who is sitting under the canopy.   *Author's Collection.*

The success of the Five-Year Plan can now be evaluated and it is evident that it achieves success:

1. Enhanced the fleet with 116 streamlined trams of better and safer types

2. The losses of bus operation had been turned into a modest profit

3. A total credit balance of £250,407 was provided during the scheme

4. There were no staff redundancies and wages were increased by 11% with 12 paid holidays a year, compared with 6 in 1933!

5. Fares had not been increased during the five years and concessions were provided

6. The public did benefit from a 100% better service and the fleet mileage was increased to 8,670,000 compared with 4 million in 1933.

Thus by 1939 the fleet stood at 160 buses and 212 trams making a total of 372 vehicles. Undoubtedly Walter Luff was favoured by modernising at a time when costs and wages were much less than the equivalent today. Thus he showed the Transport World how a fleet could be renewed virtually out of the revenue, once that had risen from increasing passengers. Therefore its achievements gave Blackpool a system to be proud of and one which carried it forward to the future dark days of the war and the post-war years which followed.

Fare Stages

Fare stages on the four main routes as used in 1961 before abandonments. The promenade route still uses the same fare stage structure.

Service 1 - North Station and Fleetwood

Out	In	
9		North Station
10		Eaves Street
11	44	Gynn Square
12	43	Cabin
13	42	Miners' Home
14	41	Bispham
15	40	Norbreck
16	39	Little Bispham
17	38	Anchorsholme Crossing
18	37	Cleveleys
19	36	Thornton Gate
20	35	Rossall Beach
21	34	Rossall Station
22	33	Rossall Square
23	32	Broadwater
24	31	Lingfield Road (Engine Sheds)
25	30	Stanley Road
26	29	Ash Street
-	28	Church Street
-	27	Fleetwood Ferry

Till 27th October 1963

Service 3 - Squires Gate - Bispham*

Out	In	
1	-	Squires Gate
2	-	Highfield Road
3	51	Watson Road
5	50	Royal Oak
6	49	Manchester Square
7	48	Central Pier
8	47	Central Station
9	46	Talbot Square
10	45	Pleasant Street
11	44	Gynn Square
12	43	Cabin
-	42	Miners' Home
-	41	Bispham Station

*Certain to Thornton Gate
Till 29th October, 1961

Service 2 - Promenade, Starr Gate and Fleetwood

Out	In	
1	-	Starr Gate
2	-	Harrowside
3	51	Pleasure Beach
5*	50	Waterloo Road
6	49	Manchester Square
7	48	Central Pier
8	47	Central Station (Tower)
9	46	Talbot Square
10	45	Pleasant Street
11	44	Gynn Square
12	43	Cabin
13	42	Miners' Home
14	41	Bispham
15	40	Norbreck
16	39	Little Bispham
17	38	Anchorsholme Crossing
18	37	Cleveleys
19	36	Thornton Gate
20	35	Rossall Beach
21	34	Rossall Station
22	33	Rossall Square
23	32	Broadwater
24	31	Lingfield Road
25	30	Stanley Road
26	29	Ash Street
-	28	Church Street
-	27	Fleetwood Ferry

*NOTE - Stage 4 South Pier removed

Service 4 - Marton, Talbot Square - South Pier

Out	In	
1	-	South Pier
2	-	Royal Oak
3	14	Threlfall Road
4	13	Rectory Road
5	12	Preston Old Road (Depot)
6	11	Woodland Grove
7	10	Devonshire Square
-	9	Hippodrome
-	8	Talbot Square

Till 28th October, 1962

ROUND BLACKPOOL BY TRAM

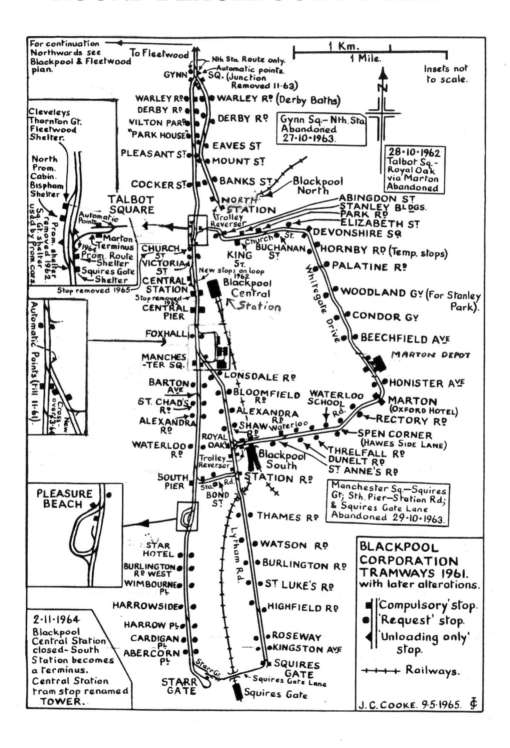

TRAMCAR SERVICES

Cars shown in the tables below are "service" cars - those cars which run with scheduled time cards. Many "specials" are run as required, mainly on Promenade.

SUMMER SEASON 1961

SERVICE NUMBER	DUTY NOS.	ROUTE OPERATED	FREQUENCY	DEPOT	CARS
1	1-9	North Station and Fleetwood	10 minutes	Bispham	9
1	10-13	North Station and Cleveleys	10 minutes	Bispham	4
2	71-83	Starr Gate and Fleetwood	10 minutes	Rigby Road	13
2	22-30	Starr Gate and Thornton Gate	10 minutes	Rigby Road	9
3	51-57	Squires Gate and Bispham	10 minutes	B ispham	7
3	58-63	Squires Gate and Cabin	10 minutes	Rigby Road	6
4	33-44	Talbot Square and Royal Oak	4 minutes	Marton	} 12
4	33-44	Talbot Square and South Pier	12 minutes	Marton	

Total Number of Service Cars: 60

Added to this, as many as 60 or 70 "specials" could be on the road, including cars operating on the Circular Tour, Fleetwood and Cleveleys, Squires Gate and Talbot Square peak hour services.

Last Trams on Converted Routes

LAST CAR	DATE	ROUTE	REPLACEMENT
Standard 154	19th October, 1936	Talbot Square and Layton	Bus Services 22-23 Marton Depot & Layton.
Unknown	19th October, 1936	Talbot Square and Central Station via Marton	
E.E. r/c/2 268	29th October, 1961	Squires Gate and Cabin	Bus Service 12 Tram: Harrowside & Cabin.
E.E. r/c/1 201	29th October, 1961	Squires Gate and Bispham	
E.E. r/c/1 205	29th October, 1961	South Pier-Marton	Not immediately replaced
Standard 48	28th October, 1962	Royal Oak - Marton	Bus Service 26
Standard 159	28th October, 1962	Talbot Square-Marton	
Balloon d.d. 256	27th October, 1963	North Station Cabin	Bus Service 25Á Tram: Tower & Fleetwood.
Brush Car 290	27th October, 1963	North Station and Fleetwood	

BLACKPOOL & FLEETWOOD
TRAMWAY - Service 1

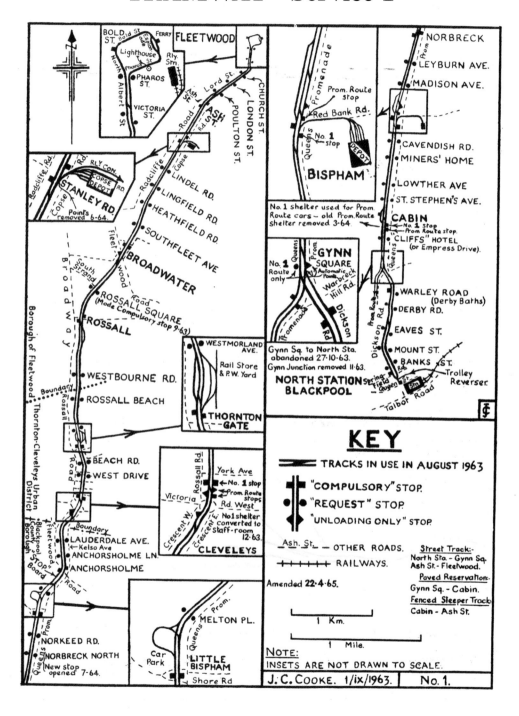

KEY

TRACKS IN USE IN AUGUST 1963

"COMPULSORY" STOP.

"REQUEST" STOP.

"UNLOADING ONLY" STOP.

Ash St. — OTHER ROADS.

++++++ RAILWAYS.

Street Track:-
North Sta. - Gynn Sq.
Ash St. - Fleetwood.

Paved Reservation:-
Gynn Sq. - Cabin.

Fenced Sleeper Track:
Cabin - Ash St.

Amended 22·4·65.

1 Km.

1 Mile.

NOTE:
INSETS ARE NOT DRAWN TO SCALE.

J. C. COOKE. 1/ix/1963.   No. 1.

A picturesque scene on 29 September 1985, with 1885 Conduit 4 leading a twenty-car procession, with its passengers in period costumes.   *Author*

Certainly the return of Dreadnought 59 between 1976 & 1990 always succeeded in attracting passengers for rides along Blackpool Promenade and even to Fleetwood! 59 was sponsored by Blackpool Civic Trust for the Centenary of the Borough in 1976 and it first stood on display on the Promenade at Foxhall and then went to Blackpool Technical College for the fundamental restoration of its body. On the 12th June 1976 Dreadnought 59 appeared on the Tower siding with costumed passengers of Civic Trust to witness the Centenary processions passing. The famous Les Dawson once recorded on the top deck of the Dreadnought and it also commenced the first Tram Sunday at Fleetwood in 1985. In this year it was the Centenary of the Promenade Tramway and consequently 1885 ex-conduit car 4 returned to Blackpool having been restored to its original appearance as a conduit car. Thus it had no trolley and was powered by batteries concealed under the longitudinal seats of the saloon. On the 29th September car 4, with all of its passengers wearing traditional costumes, led a procession of twenty trams from Talbot Square to Pleasure Beach. Followed by Dreadnought 59, there were thirteen different Blackpool trams and six from other cities, Edinburgh 35, Dublin-Howth 10, Manchester 765, Glasgow 1297, Sheffield 513, Bolton 66 and surprisingly steam tram engine "John Bull" of 1885. Undoubtedly this was the most memorable occasion on the tramway, watched by thousands of people who afterwards took rides. In that year the newly restored open-topper 706 was named by the royal "Princess Alice" and it can still be seen to this day and also features on the cover of this book!

Of the other two historic cars of the B & F Tramroad both duly returned to Blackpool on special occasions. Box 40 first returned from Heaton Park in Manchester where it had been since 1979 and was more thoroughly restored in being repanelled, rewired and retyred before its arrival in 1988. In traditional livery, 40 was sponsored by local "Fisherman's Friend" and led the Tram Sunday procession in 1988. Seen with Dreadnought 59 until 1990 the contrasting pair provided a reminder of the history when their tramways were merged in 1920. Box 40 returned to NTM Crich in 1991, was on exhibition for a short time and then went into store. However, with the Centenary in 1998, 40 returned for restoration in April 1996 and was repainted in the traditional livery, complete with "BLACKPOOL & FLEETWOOD ELECTRIC TRAMROAD" in gold letters. To complete this historic Centenary the NTM completely restored B & F Crossbench-car 2 and Pantograph-saloon 167 ready for their return to Blackpool on 22 June 1998. During the short time that they were in Blackpool they were exhibited on the depot Open Day. Also 2 & 40 commemorated the opening of the Blackpool & Fleetwood line on 1st July, with crowds of children cheering their arrival in Lord Street, as in 1898. Undoubtedly this was an epic occasion, along with a procession of trams from Pleasure Beach to Fleetwood on 12 July, thus celebrating the survival of the inter-urban tramway for 100 years!

Central Promenade with thousands of spectators watching the Centenary tramcar procession, showing Dreadnought 59, Standard 40, Princess Alice 706, Pantograph 176, 641 and many others.

Author

Open Day at the Depot with the two Blackpool & Fleetwood Tramroad Company cars 2 & 40 standing next to each other, for the first time since 1963!   Author

In 1998, 2 and 40 re-creating the original first arrival of a tram in Fleetwood on 1 July 1898, and greeted by a large crowd of local children cheering, as it happened then.

Author

OMO 4 in its plum-and-custard livery in 1972.

OUT!

"Princess Alice" 706, newly-painted in 2003 and fitted with the traditional windscreen hoods, here seen filled with passengers and passing the magnificent former Miners' Home.
Author

Very appropriate, a trawler Cevic arrives at Fleetwood Ferry, as tram 633 on 9 December 2001. Brush car 633 was reconstructed as trawler Cevic in 2000, and was sponsored by Fisherman's Friend. While looking different from a normal service car, 633 can be used on the Fleetwood service, so that it should always be run with its bows at the front. Thus the saloon seats are fixed facing forwards. While it is uni-directional, it is important that Cevic is not run stern-first!
Author

Passing the Tower, and on the main service to Starr Gate.   Author

ABOUT

CAR TYPES 1965-2004

A delightful picture of Standard-balcony 40 at Fleetwood Ferry in August 1985, with driver Ron Batter, the Mayor with his family and Transport Manager Derek Hyde with his wife.

Author

Standards

BUILT: 1923-1929. BUILDER: Blackpool Corporation Transport Dept.

BODY: As built, double-deck open-balcony unvestibuled cars of traditional design and capacity 78 passengers. Seats for 32 were provided in the lower saloon with a combination of longitudinal and transverse cushioned seats and 46 upstairs with wooden transverse seats in the saloon and curved-bench seats on the balconies. A four-window saloon with a tudor-arch effect was inherited from the "Motherwell" cars 42-43 of 1902 and characterised these cars. Twenty-two new Standards were constructed, beginning with cars 99 and 100 in 1923. In addition, thirty-three cars of older types were constructed by B.C.T. to bring the total of Standard cars up to a maximum of fifty-five. New cars were built as follows:-

99-100 built 1923 B.C.T.	150-152 built 1925 Hurst Nelson
142-143 built 1924 B.C.T	153-155 built 1926 B.C.T.
144-145 built 1925 B.C.T.	156-160 built 1927 B.C.T.
146-149 built 1924 Hurst Nelson	177 built 1929 B.C.T.

TRUCKS:	Preston McGuire equal-wheel bogies, 4ft 1in. wheel base and 30in diameter wheels.
MOTORS:	B.T.H. B.510
BRAKING:	Hand-wheel and reheostatic. 147 now fitted with air-brakes.
COLLECTOR:	Trolley boom with 4 in. swivel-head. 147 now has 6 in. head.
DIMENSIONS:	Length: 33ft. 10.in, height: 16ft. 7 in., width: 7ft. 2in.

MODIFICATIONS: Certain new Standards were fitted with Hurst Nelson maximum traction bogies at the outset. The first cars were vestibuled in March 1929, and in September of the following year, 159 became the first totally-enclosed car along with 100. 158 was one of a further six cars authorised for totally enclosing in 1930. Vestibuled open balcony cars 147, 150, 151, 160 & 177 ran until the war period, when their balconies were enclosed. These replaced cars 46 and 50, which were scrapped after accidents. 158 & 159 were decorated with lights in 1959 and thereafter operated as illuminated cars at night, but in daylight as ordinary passenger cars.

OPERATION: Standards ran on all routes in the town with exception of the Fleetwood route. In 1935-6 new streamlined "Balloons" replaced Standards on the Gynn Square & Squire Gate via Lytham Road service. Standards were then confined to Layton, Marton, Central Drive and South Pier group of routes, and peak-hour extras on the Promenade. Following the abandonment of the Layton and Central Drive routes in October 1936, only fourteen Standards were required for the Marton service during the winter season, and these were the all enclosed type. The starting of WW II in 1939 prevented the purchase of fifteen shorter Balloons for the Marton route, and thus the Standard remained in service. Following the relaying of this track in 1948, new rolling stock in the form of sun-saloon "Vambac" cars 10 – 21 were introduced to the route, replacing Standards. However, it was not until 1952 that the Standards lost their scheduled duties to south Pier, when six railcoaches were transferred from the Promenade duties, after the arrival of the Coronations. 24 Standards were scrapped in Blundell St Depot, and a further six at Thornton Gate in 1958, leaving eight for Promenade use, until their finale in1996 with 147, 158, & 159. Balcony 40 returned from National Tramway Museum for Centenary in 1985. 147 returned form USA in October 2000 needing restoration. It was launched on 3 April 2002.

Tour of Illuminations by Standard 147, having been beautifully restored by Blackpool Transport Services upon its return from U.S.A in October 2000, thus it first appeared in 2002.   *Bryan Grint.*

An impressive assembly at Fleetoood Ferry on 11 May 1985, with Pantograph 167, Manchester
California 765 and Jubilee 761, in the Tramway Centenary year. Author

Pantograph Cars 167-176

BUILT: 1928

BUILDER: English Electric, Dick Kerr Works, Preston.

BODY: Single-deck "Pullman" cars, with enclosed platforms providing rear
entrance and exit. Purchased at £2,000 each for use on the Blackpool and
Fleetwood tramroad. The design reflects the inter-urban nature of the line, and
follows American, rather than British, practice. A clerestory roof is a feature of
the saloon, which seats 44 on upholstered transverse seats, with two fixed seats
on each platform, making a total of 48. A route-box was originally fitted on the
roof at each end, which displayed destination initials, like "F" for Fleetwood. The
notable feature was the pantograph collector by Brecknell, Munro & Rogers,
mounted on a tall tower. Car 167 was delivered on Monday, 30 July 1928 and the
others arrived at intervals thereafter, 174-176 actually arriving early in 1929.

TRUCKS:	Dick Kerr equal-wheel bogies (McGuire type) until 1950, then E.E. 1939 type from Sunsaloons 10-21, apart from 167 which retains the original ones.
MOTORS:	G.E.C. WT 28L H.P.: 40 x 2 (167 has B.T.H. 265 motors).
CONTROLLERS:	B.T.H. B. 510
BRAKING:	Air-wheel brakes by Westinghouse, hand-wheel, rheostatic.
COLLECTOR:	Pantograph mounted on tall-tower, removed after five years and replaced by trolley-pole with rope, and the tower shortened.
DIMENSIONS:	Length: 40 feet, width: 7ft 6in, platform-entrance 5ft 6in.

MODIFICATIONS: Various alterations have taken place structurally since new. The pantograph collector was removed because of sand interfering with the lubrication and the unsuitability of the overhead line along the Promenade restricting them to the North Station route. Route boxes were replaced by indicator boxes in 1929-30. During 1936-7 they were redesigned to bring them into line with modern trams, by the fitting of platform doors, larger metal windscreens, and curved moulding round the indicator boxes. They were then painted in all-cream livery with green lining. Bogies from 10-21 were fitted to all cars except 167, which became a permanent way car in 1954. After passenger-flow alterations to the body, 176 was scrapped in the same year. Remaining cars used on summer-service until 1960. 172 and 175 made the last passenger journeys at Easter 1962 without their trolley ropes in order to use the new trolley-reverser!

OPERATION: Operated almost exclusively on North Station and Fleetwood service and short-workings to Thornton Gate, running from Bispham Depot.

SITUATION: All these cars were withdrawn from passenger service after Easter 1961 (see cars scrapped and preserved lists). 168 was withdrawn in May 1961 top become The Rocket illuminated tram, 174 became the trailer for The Western Train in 1962. 170 became the works car in January 1962 and converted to HMS Blackpool in April 1965. Preserved 167 returned to Blackpool for the Centenary in 1985 and in 1998 for Centenary of B & F Tramroad. The Rocket has been given to LTT, Western Train was displayed on Tram Sunday 2003 and HMS Blackpool has been rebuilt in 2003/04 for new use.

A striking scene of 167 in North Albert Street on 11 May 1985 in the hands of The Author!   Tony Stevenson

English Electric Railcoaches.
Series 1. 200-224

BUILT: 1933-34

BUILDER: English Electric Company, Preston.

BODY: Single-deck centre-entrance cars based upon the revolutionary design of prototype 200, which had been originally designed for the overseas market. Under the General Manager Walter Luff's Five Year Plan of Modernisation, 24 cars like 200 were ordered. They were designed to replace the old B & F ex-Company saloon cars and offered new standards of passenger comfort. 48 transverse, reversible and cushioned seats were provided, floor heaters were fitted and an electric clock in each saloon. The driver was seated in his own cab, while the safety of passengers were ensured by folding doors on the platform. In each saloon there were sliding-opening sunshine-roof panels.

TRUCKS:	English Electric equal-wheel bogies, 4ft. wheelbase.
MOTORS:	English Electric 305. H.P.: 57 X 2
CONTROLERS:	E.E. type Z.4
BRAKING:	Westinghouse air-wheel, hand-wheel and rhetostatic.
COLLECTOR:	Trolley boom mounted on a tower. 200 was fitted with a pantograph at Preston and briefly at Blackpool. Cars fitted with a 6in. wheel swivel-headed trolleys, when running from Marton Depot.
DIMENSIONS:	Length: 43ft 3in, over fenders. Width: 7ft 6in.

FURTHER NOTES: With remarkably few changes, these cars gave staunch service for over thirty years - from their introduction in 1934 until their general withdrawal from service on 27 October 1963, with the closure of the North Station route. Car 200 had been delivered in June 1933 and 224 in February 1934. Latterly, cars 214 and 224 had their sliding "sunshine" roofs removed.

Railcoach 214 in Talbot Square destined for Royal Oak in 1962. It has been rebuilt without the side indicators and the sunshine roofs, and thus looks less domed at each end.   *Author.*

Vambac 208 in service outside Marion Depot in 1952, showing its distinct appearance of higher-standing with the flares. Notice the Scout bus and ambulance following.   *R. B. Parr NTM*

OPERATION: Railcoaches were operated on all routes and from three depots and latterly they provided the basic service on North Station and Squires Gate routes. Each depot had its allocation, lower range of numbers being at Bispham.

SITUATION: 206 was the first car to be scrapped on 22 September 1961, after a collision with a Coronation at Gynn Square. This series decreased with the conversion to bus operation of the three tram street-routes by 1963. 224 became a Permanent Way car in October 1964 but was restored to service in May 1965, being the only one of its class in operation. 221 became Engineering Car on 21 April 1965 and 220 was stored in Blundell Street depot. In 1972 these three became OMO cars: 224 (610) - 3, 220 (608) - 4, 221 (609) - 5.

VAMBAC RAILCOACH 208

This car in December 1946 became the first Blackpool "Vambac" car, being experimentally fitted with the multi-notch accelerator in the base of its tower, and enclosed by masking fitted with shades for ventilation. Also it was fitted with amber glass above its windscreens, thus making it distinctive in appearance.

                TRUCKS: Maley & Taunton. HS. 44 with track brakes.
                MOTORS: Crompton Parkinson C92. H.P.: 45 x 4.
           CONTROLLERS: Crompton Parkinson "Vambac"
                BRAKING: Air-disc, magnetic-track, remote-control rheostatic,
                         hand-disc.
              OPERATION: Ran from Marton Depot on this route after initial
                         experiments.
              SITUATION: Scrapped at Marton Depot in March 1963.

Open Boat Cars 225-236
Now 600-607

BUILT: 1934-35

BUILDER: English Electric, Preston

BODY: Designed by the General Manager, Walter Luff, these cars were intended to have all the advantages of the Toastracks without the disadvantages of the running-boards. Consequently, it has a centre-entrance, over which is a canopy supporting the trolley tower and containing four indicators and signal bells. The open saloons have sides reaching to seat-top level and 56 seats wooden-slatted and reversible. The body is of composite construction with an underframe of rolled-steel sections, teak framework and steel panels. 225 being the trial car, differs in having lower sides. Flares at each end are lined with beading and the platforms have half-height swing doors.

TRUCKS:	English Electric equal-wheel, 4ft wheelbase.
MOTORS:	E.E. 327. H.P: 40 x 2
CONTROLLERS:	E.E. D.B.I.: Cars 225, 226, 236
	B.T.H. B.18: Cars 227-235. Today - all E.E. Z6.
BRAKING:	Westinghouse air-wheel, rheostatic, hand-wheel.
COLLECTOR:	Trolley boom and swivel-head till 1962,
	now fixed-head trolley.
DIMENSIONS:	42ft 4in in length, width 7ft 6in.

MODIFICATIONS: In 1958, car 227 was fitted with a light windscreen and during this and the following year, windscreens were fitted to all the Boat cars. By 1990, these were replaced by new twin windscreens of toughened glass. Pantographs were fitted to 602 and 604 in 1992 but found hazardous for passengers, whose clothes were stained. Trolleys were thus restored.

OPERATION: All these cars were based at Marton Depot and operated the Circular Tour and Promenade "specials". When it closed in 1962, four Boats went to Blundell St. Depot and eight went to Bispham Depot where they operated in 1963 on the Promenade Circulars and "specials". In 1964 Boats finally transferred to Rigby Road Depot, where they are today.

A line of Three trams in Talbot Square during June 1934, with 225 waiting for The Circular Tour and Standards on the Marton and Layton services.   *M. J. O'Connor NTM*

SITUATION: In April 1968, 229, 231, 232, 234 were scrapped in Blundell Street Depot as surplus to requirements. In 1971, 226 (601) went to San Francisco for the British Trade Festival and on to the Rio Vista Museum in California. 228 (603) went to Philadelphia for U.S.A. Bi-centennial Celebrations and gave city-centre tours on 5ft 3in gauge track. It returned in 1978, was disused until it departed for San Francisco permanently in 1985. Here it is operated by MUNI as a British tram in the historic international fleet. In 1986, 606 operated at the Glasgow Garden Festival and in 2000 went to Trolleyville, U.S.A. in exchange for Standard 147. It now operates in Cleveland, making a trio of Boats in the U.S.A.! Thus there are now five Boat cars in Blackpool: 600 in the original livery, 605 in the wartime fleet livery, 604 in Eighties livery, 602 in yellow and black livery, 607 in yellow and green, advertising Blackpool Transport tickets.

Little Bispham with a Boat heading for Cleveleys,
R. P .Fergusson

Former Open-Top Balloons 237-249, now 700-712

BUILT: 1934.

BUILDER: English Electric, Preston

BODY: Introduced by Walter Luff to replace the Dreadnoughts, these cars were a modern version of the traditional seaside open-topper. The body and bogies were manufactured in Preston and the traction equipment in Bradford. Steel shutter blinds could close the staircases during poor weather and make the car a single-decker. Entrance to the platform was by two-piece folding doors. Each saloon seated 20 on upholstered transverse seats, while on the open-top deck, 54 teak wooden-slatted seats were provided and bench seats at each end, totalling 94. The body has a teak frame, built on an underframe of welded rolled steel. The trolley was supported by a gantry arch in the centre of the upper deck.

TRUCKS: E..E. equal-wheel bogies, 4ft 9in wheelbase, wheels 27in diameter.
MOTORS: E.E. 305. H.P. 57 x 2
CONTROLLERS: E.E. Z6. Designed to increase the running-speed of double-deckers from the 24mph for town and Promenade running to 35mph on the 8th field-shunt position.
BRAKING: Westinghouse air-wheel, rheostatic - 8 notches, hand-wheel.
COLLECTOR: Trolley boom on 700 & 706. Pantographs on the others.
DIMENSION: Length 42ft 3in, width 8ft 6in centre doorway. 4ft 6in.

MODIFICATIONS: Car 237 was delivered on 6 February 1934 and displayed at Talbot Square as 226, with Boat 225. It was renumbered 237 - the first of thirteen open-toppers - to fit in a dozen Boat cars as 225-236. Certainly 237 has a most vertical front, which was changed to more sloping on the others. During the war, in 1941 and 1942, the top decks of these cars were enclosed in the style of 250-263 and the end bench seats were removed, reducing the capacity to 84. These could always be identified without the windscreen hoods, a more flat roof and the thinly-upholstered wooden seats on the upper-deck. Today, these have been replaced by upholstered seats and the bench seats restored, now seating 94. The subsequent changes are shared by all Balloons (see opposite).

SITUATION: In July 1980, following the collision between 705 & 706, 705 was scrapped in 1982 but 706 was rebuilt in the open-top condition in 1985. It was originally fitted with a short roof in the centre and a pantograph, but now it has a trolley. In 2003, it was repainted in original style and windscreen hoods fitted. At Easter, 1997, prototype 700 was rebuilt in the 1942 form, with twin indicators and windscreens in the green and cream lined livery, complete with a trolley. In 2003, it was repainted again and the original windscreen hoods were fitted. 707 and 709 have been rebuilt in a new-style with single windscreens and new fitted hopper-windows and modern seating, but retain centre-entrance and staircases.

A busy scene of three Balloons at Cleveleys in 1978, with first-series 701 & 708 and second-series 713 in the centre, being distinguished by its front dome.   *Author.*

A profile of 721 at Pleasure Beach, showing the new livery of the Eighties and the raked-style of the body.
Author

Double-deck Balloons 250-263
Now 713-726

BUILT: 1934-35

BUILDER: English Electric, Preston

BODY: Similar in specification to the open-toppers, the first of these cars was on exhibition in the English Electric Works at Preston on 3 December 1934, along with modern cars from Sunderland, Belfast, Leeds and trolleybuses from Bradford. 250 arrived in Blackpool on 10 December 1934 and most of the fourteen cars of this type had been delivered by Easter 1935, each costing £3,500. They had seating for 84 passengers, with 20 in each saloon and 44 on the upper deck. Heating was provided by thermostatically-controlled radiators through grills at floor level. Ventilation was by half-drop windows and in the upper saloon there were two 6ft sliding roof panels. Ceilings comprised Alhambrinal panels, and lighting was provided each side behind curved glass lines in art-deco.

MODIFICATIONS: These cars were distinguished from 237-249 by the trolley-arch over the roof, which supports the trolley and allowed the sunshine roofs to slide open. 250 was fitted with fluorescent lighting in 1946. Modification to single indicator display using fibreglass moulding, began with car 257 in June 1955, and proceeded until 722 (259) in 1980. All cars were increased to 94 seating, by adding bench seats at each end of the upper saloon. Sunshine roofs were removed along with the trolley-arch, culminating with 722 in 1980.

OPERATION: Balloons of both series operated on Squires Gate service in summer and winter until 1951, when all double-deckers were withdrawn from winter service. Subsequently, operation was confined to the Squires Gate service in summer until 1961, when the route was converted to buses. In 1958 Balloons operated to Fleetwood for the first time, when the track was fitted with check-rail. In 1971, they operated Fleetwood and Starr Gate service for the first time during the season. This continued until 2002 and may resume in 2004.

SITUATION: 725 and 714 were rebuilt in a new style and renumbered 761 and 762 (see page 58). 718 & 724 have been rebuilt in a new square-ended style, with fixed seats and hopper windows, but retain centre-entrance and staircases.

E.E. Railcoaches Series 2
264-283 and then 611-620

BUILT: On 28 January 1935, a tender for a further twenty railcoaches was accepted from the English Electric Company and these cars became 264-283. In specification they are the same as the cars of the first series with the exception that they were fitted with the improved E.E. Z6 controllers.

MODIFICATIONS: Half of these railcoaches, 272-281, were rebuilt as towing cars for the new trailers, which arrived in 1960 (see page 50). In 1965, the remaining railcoaches were having the sliding sunshine roof removed, which gave them a flat roof. During the winter of 1963, they were also fitted with fan heaters mounted centrally over the entrance to each saloon. A new three-colour livery was adopted also: cream panels, green above and an orange tower.

OPERATION: Originally operating Starr Gate and Fleetwood route, they were replaced by Coronations in 1953. Then they were mostly allocated to Marton and Rigby Road Depots and used on Squire Gate route until 1961 and Marton route until 1962. Notable in the latter connection were cars 265, 266, 269, 282, 283, which were fitted with swivel-head trolleys. They transferred to the Fleetwood route in October 1962 and were then used on Fleetwood and Cleveleys local service during winter 1963.

SITUATION: In 1966, 264 was rebuilt with the towing-car appearance and panelled in ICI Darvic plastic. In 1968, 618 (271) was rebuilt with a longer body seating 56 and with tapering ends. This started the appearance of the OMO cars. In 1972, 616 (269) was thus rebuilt to become the first OMO (see opposite).

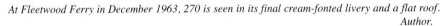

At Fleetwood Ferry in December 1963, 270 is seen in its final cream-fonted livery and a flat roof.
Author.

A 1972 trial run for OMO 3 in the original livery and showing new features of the body, including door switches on the outside. *The Gazette.*

Railcoaches became OMOs 1-13

MODIFICATIONS: Commencing with 616, the body was lengthened by a tapered platform at each end, making it 49 feet. Entrances were at the front, while the centre doors were retained as exits. The driver position was thus on the right-hand side, the controller to be used with the right hand. Saloons were fitted with back-to-back fixed seats and new windows with "hopper" ventilators, and a through centre aisle with steps down to centre doors. The roof tapered to the single indicator screen at each end. The initial livery was unusual sunshine yellow and a maroon roof. Bogies were rebuilt with metalastik suspension, starting with 10 in April 1975 - which commenced a new red and cream livery!

1972: 1-616, 2-620, 3-610, 4-608, 5-609
1973: 617-6, 619-7
1974: 612-8, 613-9
1975: 614-10, 615-11, 611-12
1976: 618-13
All became red and cream in livery.

OPERATION: OMOs went into service on the Starr Gate - Fleetwood route in 1972 and throughout the year provided the basic fleet, until the new Centenary class began to replace them in 1984. They were deemed to be more economical with a crew of one, and had a capacity of 48 seated + 16 standing. However, they were not popular trams, and became known by crews as "coffins".

SITUATION: The use of the OMO's ceased in February 1993, with 5. 11 was used for trials with bogie for a new articulated car. OMO 7 was rebuilt in the form of a Vanguard crossbench car 619 in 1987. In 2004, three remain in existence: 8 owned by LTT and in-store at Blackpool. 5 owned by NTM and in-store at Clay Cross, while 10 functions as a café in Reading.

Trailer Towing Cars 272-281
Now 671-680

BUILT: 1935

BUILDER: English Electric   REBUILT: 1959-61 BCT Works

BODY: 276 & 275 were rebuilt in 1957-58 as towing-car and trailer. This unit made its inaugural run to Fleetwood on 9 April 1958, after extensive tests and Ministry approval being received. Based on experience gained with this unit, ten new trailers were ordered and reconstruction of railcoaches commenced in 1959. These cars were transformed in appearance to resemble the Coronations, use being made of aluminium for panels and resin-bonded fibre-glass for roof and mouldings. Lightweight folding-doors were fitted and operated by Peter's electro-pneumatic equipment; lights in the driver's cab indicated when they were open. Curved roof lights were rubber-mounted and fitted flush with the roof, while each end had an indicator-box with "Progress Twin-car" panel above destinations. Willison automatic couplings were fitted at each end. The saloons were lightened by the use of "Panax" laminated plastic, and the whole effect represented complete transformation. They appeared in service as follows:

1960: 277, 272 280, (272, 276 and 277 used in summer 1960).

1961: 279, 273, 278, 275 (the latter being converted from a trailer in March), 274. All cars were finished in an all-cream livery with green linings initially.

TECHNICAL DETAILS: As for E.E. railcoaches, series 1 & 2.

MODIFICATIONS: Cars 281 & T1 permanently coupled in 1963, with driver's cab fitted in the trailer and removed form 281, thus making the capacity 53 + 61.Thus the twin-car unit was able to use crossovers and make it reversible. Improved break-away connections fitted between the two cars, allowing for disconnection of power cables in the event of a coupling fracture. Air hoses removed from leading ends of towing-car, and cars repainted in new half green and cream livery. Seven sets were completed in this way until 677 & 687 (277/T7) in 1970. Upon overhaul in 1969, 676 lost its sunshine roof and rear indicator boxes, having a plain rear dome. However, 675 retained its sunshine roof until 1980, when it was removed along with roof lights. 672, 674, 676 have been mounted on bogies with "Metalastik" rubber suspension, from OMOs.

OPERATION: Prototype set ran on Coastal Tour at first, other sets operated limited-stop services between Starr Gate or Pleasure Beach and Little Bispham or Fleetwood. In 1965, the coupled-sets commenced a Pleasure Beach and Bispham service. In 2003, the twin-cars operated Starr Gate and Fleetwood service for the first time, but they did slow-down the service time!

SITUATION: From winter 1970, 678-680 were operated separately and reconnected with trailers in the Season. From September, 1972, they have operated as railcoaches. 678 was the first tram fitted with Brecknell Willis pantograph in 1975. New liveries in Metro bus-route colours were introduced to the first four twin-cars in 2003, showing the coastal-line stops along each side.

Trailer Cars T1-T10
Now 681-690

For the first time T1 is towed by 277 to the Tower, having been presented by M. C. W. to the Mayor of Blackpool..
                                                                                          The Gazette

BUILT: 1960

BUILDER: Metropolitan Cammel-Weymann Ltd., Birmingham

BODY: Single-deck centre-entrance, two saloons seating 66 on transverse reversible upholstered seats. Lightweight construction featured use of aluminium panelling and fibreglass mouldings. "Auster" half-drop ventilators fitted in second and fourth windows and Peter's electro-pneumatic folding platform doors. The saloon has an extremely pleasing finish with linoleum floor coverings, "Panax" panels, window framings of pressed aluminium finished in stove-enamel and ceiling panels of patterned "Alhambrinal". Roof windows are provided for the benefit of standing passengers and lighting strips are fitted next to these. T1 was delivered on Saturday, 16 July 1960, connected to 277 for presentation and used for inaugural run on 25 July. Other cars were delivered at intervals, with T9 and T10 arriving in January 1961 to complete the delivery.

TRUCKS: Maley & Taunton equal-wheel bogies, wheelbase 5ft 6in steel wheels 27in. Construction: outside-framed, hornwayless, rubber-springing.

CONTROLLERS: Cars T1-T7 were fitted with E.E. Z6 controller at one end.

BRAKING: Air-wheel to all wheels, separate hand-brake in trailer.

DIMENSIONS: Length: 43ft 10in, width: 7ft 6in, Height 9ft 11in.

MODIFICATIONS: T1 linked with 281 in 1963 and had a waist-height partition for a driver's cab. Cars T2-T7 have a complete partition and capacity is reduced to 61. Headlights were fitted to the leading-end of these cars and a new painting livery was applied to twin cars, of half green and cream.

OPERATION: See Trailer Towing Cars on facing page.

SITUATION: 688 (T8) was scrapped in 1982 as surplus. 689 & 690 sold to G.E.C. in 1981 for experimental purposes, and tried at Kearsley. Then sent to Bradford Transport Museum which closed in 1989 and 689 and 690 were scrapped.

Two Brush cars 300 & 288 with the new single indicators passing on Cleveleys Orion curve in January 1964. They have contrasting liveries; cream-fronted 300 and 288 with an orange tower.

(Opposite) Vambac 303 at Cleveleys in 1962, having reversed lor North Station. Notice the ventilators beneath the trolley tower tor the Vambac equipment, and its M & T bogies.

Author.

Brush Cars 284-303 now 621-638

BUILT: 1937

BUILDER: Brush Company, Loughborough

BODY: Single-deck saloon body with centre entrances and a big improvement in appearance over the English Electric railcoaches. These cars were fitted with air-operated sliding doors by G.D. Peters of Slough, which could be operated by the driver. Forty-eight cushioned reversible seats were provided in the saloons, and two folding seats on the platform, making the total 50. Platform seats were an insurance risk and so were removed early. The driver had a pedestal seat in each cab.   Stainless steel moulding on the side panels provided a streamlined appearance, together with the flares on each front. A Sunbeam sliding roof was fitted in each saloon and finished in alhambrinal, All the windows were Widney winding full-drop types. Saloon lighting was provided in panels at each side above the windows and these showed from the outside through slender green panels. The floor covering was two-colour linoleum and Electroway tubular heaters were fitted. The final touch to elegant appearance were square clocks, mounted over the driver's doors in each saloon.

TRUCKS: E.M.B. hornless equal-wheel bogies, 4ft 3in wheelbase 27in wheels. These bogies were specially designed for a low-loading car, with the side frames swept up over the axle boxes, which were mounted on the long laminated springs.

MOTORS: Crompton Parkinson C162 (now E.E. 305) H.P. 57 x 2.
CONTROLLERS: Crompton Parkinson CTJ (now E.E. Z4)
BRAKING: Air-wheel E.M.B. rheostatic and hand-wheel
COLLECTOR: Trolley-boom (now pantograph) mounted on tower.
DIMENSIONS: Length 42ft 3in, width: 7ft 6in.

MODIFICATIONS: All cars were fitted with single indicator boxes at each end, beginning with 288 in 1958, and ending with 284 (621) in 1980. All other cars had sliding sunshine roofs removed after transfer to Rigby Road Depot in October 1963, and air-operated sliding doors were replaced by folding doors. Fan heaters were fitted to the saloons of all cars in winter 1963, but the original floor heaters had been disused for some years, Car 301 had fluorescent lighting dating from 1947. All cars were re-equipped with English Electric motors and Z4 controllers from scrapped railcoaches. 638 (302) was rebuilt for one-man operation with front entrances and in all-cream livery 1970-3 but was ineffective.

OPERATION: Initially operated from Rigby Road Depot, until transferred to Bispham Depot in 1940. Used mainly on the North Station and Fleetwood route and some Promenade duties. Operated on Squires Gate and Bispham service in Summer from 1958 to 1961. All cars are now in service from Rigby Road Depot on the Starr Gate and Fleetwood service, mainly in the summer season.

SITUATION: Thirteen Brush cars are still in regular service, many covered with adverts. 633 was rebuilt in 2001 as an illuminated trawler CEVIC FD 241. Of the other seven cars: 635 (298) was preserved for restoration in 1974 by NTM in its original condition. 624 & 628 became used as permanent-way unit from 1971. The other four scrapped: 303-1963, 301-1968, 292-1980, 302-1984.

VAMBAC BRUSH CAR 303

An experimental car with 208 in 1946, using conventional controllers and Maley & Taunton HS44 bogies. By 1953 it was fully-fitted with "Vambac" equipment and while 303 was tried on the Marton route, the air-doors slowed it down, and thus it was returned to Bispham Depot, where it was unique.

TRUCKS:	Maley & Taunton H.S.44 without track brakes.
MOTORS:	Crompton Parkinson C92. H.P.: 45 x 4
CONTROLLERS:	Crompton Parkinson "Vambac"
BRAKING:	Air-disc, remote-control rheostatic, hand-disc
OPERATION:	303 operated from Bispham depot, largely on Promenade and occasionally on North Station route as an extra. Being different, 303 was not popular with Bispham drivers, and was thus largely in the depot.

Sunsaloons & Marton Vambacs 10-21

An ideal view of a new Sunsaloon outside Rigby Road Depot in 1939, showing the tapered-front and the open centre-roof. Notice the Coliseum Bus Station is full of coaches!
Author's Collection.

BUILT: 1939

BUILDER: English Electric, Preston.

BODY: These cars when built, were intended as a modern version of the old B & F crossbench cars which they were intended to replace. Although modern in external appearance, also representing the ultimate in pre-war design, they were built cheaply for summer use only. Old electrical equipment was used, including B.T.H. B265C motors from cars 62-68 and Marton "Box cars" 27, 29, 30 & 32, while the E.E.DBI controllers were possibly obtained from other systems. Features included wooden reversible seating, half-glazed windows, half height doors, opening soft roof, low-lighting and no partition between saloons and the driver's cabs. The first car was delivered on 14th August 1939, and passengers complained about the draughts. Semi-open cars were not much-needed during the War, but in 1942 all windows were fully-glazed, and full-length platform doors were fitted. In this state the cars became known as "cattle-trucks" by the troops, who they carried for training.

TRUCKS: E.E. equal-wheel 4ft wheel-base.
MOTORS: B.T.H. B265C H.P.: 35 x 2
CONTROLLERS: E.E. DB1
COLLECTOR: Trolley-boom fixedhead, later swivel-head - Marton
DIMENSIONS: Length 44ft, width 7ft 6in.

Autum 1962, Marton Vambac 16 and 208 are seen passing on South Station bridge in Waterloo Road, for the final weeks.   *Author*

POST-WAR RECONSTRUCTION:

BODY: After running as "cattle trucks" from 1945 to 1948, in that 10-15 were improved in body comforts and placed into service on the newly-relaid Marton route. Upholstered seats were fitted in the saloons, partitions made between driver and passengers and a centre-roof fitted for a fluorescent-light strip and cables. These improvements were carried out from 1948 until 1949, when car 15 went on to the Marton route. The cars were finished in a striking livery of green and cream, with green flares on each side and a "V" at each end. Late in 1949, car 21 appeared on the Promenade like 10-15 (which were operating on Marton route), but newly-fitted with "Vambac" equipment. All these cars went into service on the Marton route, where they replaced Standard double-deckers. The evolution of Marton Vambac cars was thus complete for 10-21 and a further six E.E. railcoaches should have been fitted with "Vambac" equipment, but it did not take place.

TRUCKS: Maley & Taunton HS44 bogies, resilient wheels, 6ft 0in wheelbase.

MOTORS: Crompton Parkinson "Vambac" (Variable Automatic Multinotch Braking & Acceleration Control).

BRAKING: Air-disc, remote-control rheostatic, hand-disc.

OPERATION: Intended for Promenade seasonal use when new, but the war changed the situation. In 1942, they were fully-glazed and used as troop-carriers from Squires Gate to Rossall rifle ranges. In 1945 they were used for Promenade "specials" again and in 1948 10-15 went into service on the Marton route. All cars of this series were in-service on Marton by 1952. Thus they were based at Marton Depot and exclusive to this route, until its closure on 28 October 1962.

SITUATION: The first to be scrapped was 10 in 1961 after a crash, another ten were broken up in Marton Depot in March 1963. 11 was salvaged in January 1963 for a final tour by historic trams. 11 operated at East Anglia Transport Museum 1969-1983 and has now been fully restored for operation - in 2004.

Newly-repainted 316 in 1955 is seen without front chrome beading, opening standee-windows, and a wider roof without the centre-glass panels. Of course, Coronations never visited NORTH STATION BLACKPOOL.
W. R. Buckley

Coronations 304-328 then 641-664

BUILT: 1952-53

Builder: Charles Roberts, Horbury

BODY: Single-deck centre-entrance car seating 56 passengers on transverse reversible cushioned seats. Of very handsome appearance, these cars followed the pre-war style in having two saloons with a centre-entrance, which subsequently precluded economies of one-man operation. The unladen weight of 19 tons made them expensive to operate, leading to broken axles at an early stage. However these cars appeared as the ultimate in British tramcar development, with their fluorescent lighting, comfortable seating, glass-panelled roof, extensive "Alhambrinal" faced panels, electro-pneumatic sliding doors and "Vambac" traction equipment. This equipment of car 304 was demonstrated at the Festival of Britain 1951, and a plaque on the car commemorated the fact. Car 304 was delivered to Blackpool on 5th June 1952 and was first driven from the North Pier to the Pleasure Beach by the Mayor and comedian Jimmy Edwards. Delivery was completed when 328 arrived on 7th January 1954.

TRUCKS: Maley & Taunton H.S. 44, equal-wheel bogie, resilient-wheels 6ft wheelbase and fitted with braking disc.
MOTORS: Crompton Parkinson C.92x4   H.P. 45x4
CONTROLLERS:Crompton Parkinson "Vambac" accelerator and braking.
BRAKING: Remote-control rheostatic, magnetic track brakes, air/hand-brake.
COLLECTOR: Trolley-pole, originally 6ins swivel head, then fixed-head.
DIMENSIONS: Length 50ft, width: 7ft 11in, height: 10ft

MODIFICATIONS: Chrome strip embellishments and sliding standee window fittings soon removed because of rusting. Green band above windows removed in livery change of 1961, and at the same time "Alhambrinal" facing painted cream, and glass roof glass panels sheeted over with aluminium, to prevent leaking. Steel side panels were replaced by aluminium panels in an attempt to cut weight. In 1964, an attempt to reduce maintenance costs and increased reliability resulted in car 323 having "Vambac" equipment removed and replaced by conventional E.E. Z6 controller, using rheostatic braking for service stops. 328 was similarly treated, followed by 310 in 1965, and all three had a new mundane livery of half-green and half-cream with an orange trolley tower. In these cars, resistances were fitted under the gantry, providing air-flow cooling. A further ten car followed: 306, 327, 324, 318, 326, 322, 325, 321, 320, ending with 319 in February 1970. Fluorescent lighting was removed and replaced by light bulbs, thus reducing their appearance.

OPERATION: Starr Gate and Fleetwood service until 1963, subsequently used for summer service until 1970, when withdrawal followed.

SITUATION: The scrapping process started with 313 in 1968, the "Vambac" equipped cars followed, and finally the re-equipped cars, completed by 1975. Three survived: 660 (324) retained by BTS, 304 & 327 were preserved. Vambac 304 returned and was restored for "Salvage Squad" TV programmes in 2003/4. A tour with 660, restored the memorable sight of Coronation cars in service again!

Coronations 660 & 304 seen together at North Pier on 8 November 2003, for the first time in thirty years - making a unique occasion!   *Author.*

762 on Pleasure Beach loop in 1983 with the Casino, showing its smart appearance with two doors. 761 can be seen on pages 4 and 40.   (Opposite)   641 passing the enormous Lewis's buliding in 1984, showing its roof-mounted advertising panels and unique pantograph tower

Author

Jubilee Cars 761 & 762

BUILT: 761 - 1979, 762 - 1982

BUILDER: Blackpool Borough Transport

BODY: Originally Balloons 725 & 714, they had been stored in Blundell Street Depot and it was decided to rebuild them in a new form with front entrance/exit, thus allowing them to be operated like OMOs, with a crew of one. Complete reconstruction of the 725 body involved the moving of the stairs to each end, thus filling the centre entrance and platform. Complete new end-sections were built, and added to the body, thus making 761 longer than a Balloon. New longer window sections were fitted flush with the body, thus totally changing its original appearance. However 761 with 98 seats was found to be slow loading and unloading through the front entrance. Thus the construction of 762 included a centre exit, and adjacent stairs, thus reducing the capacity to 90. During the subsequent body servicing of 761, it is surprising that centre exits were not fitted.

TRUCKS:	Blackpool Transport 5ft 6in wheelbase.Metalastik suspension.
MOTORS:	E.E. 305. H.P. 57 x 2
CONTROLLERS:	Brush "Chopper" control - operated by lever.
BRAKING:	"Chopper" control air-braking, hand-wheel.
COLLECTOR:	Pantograph - originally mini-sized on 761
DIMENSIONS:	Length 46ft, width 7ft 6in, wheelbase 22ft 4in.
OPERATION:	These cars have been used on the Starr Gate and Fleetwood service at all times of the year with only the driver, but in the Season also with a conductor. In 2003, they were limited to Cleveleys and Pleasure Beach service.
SITUATION:	After three versions of fleet livery on 761, it now advertises "News of the World", while 762 looks better in purple and white, advertising UNISON.

Centenary Cars. 641-648

BUILT: 1984-1988

BUILDER: East Lancs, Blackburn

BODY: It was decided in 1982, following the completion of 762, that the replacement of the OMOs should be by ten single-deck cars built by East Lancs. The dimensions would follow the size of the Coronations and 660 with wooden corners were tested for clearance. The body of 641 left the Blackburn works on 17 April 1984, was weighed at the brewery at 10.5 tonnes and with the bogies would weigh 17.5 tonnes. This new car was a more modern appearance, with front entrance and nearer exit, to facilitate the driver's supervision. However, the flat roof was surmounted by a huge illuminated advert box and a tapering tower for a pantograph. In the saloon there was fixed seating for 54, facing the centre of the car and some longitudinal seats. There was room for 20 standing passengers, thus having a capacity of 74. On the following cars, 642-648, no advert boxes were fitted and seating was 52 with 20 standing.

TRUCKS:	Blackpool Transport 5ft 6in wheelbase and Metalastik suspension.
MOTORS:	E.E. 305. H.P. 57 x 2.
CONTROLLERS:	Brush "Chopper" control - operated by lever.
BRAKING:	"Chopper" control air-braking, hand-wheel.
COLLECTOR:	Pantograph
DIMENSIONS:	Length: 51ft 6in, width: 8ft 2in, height: 9ft 4in.

OPERATION: The first trial runs for 641 took place: Promenade on 6 June, Fleetwood on 8 June and entered service on 6 July 1984. The Centenary cars operate Starr Gate and Fleetwood service throughout the year.

SITUATION: In 1985, a second Centenary car 651 appeared. It was provided by GEC Traction to test its own control equipment, and mounted on M & T HS44 bogies fitted with 4 "switched reluctance" motors. Following the trials, GEC sold the 651 to Blackpool Transport in 1988, it was re-equipped like other Centenary cars and re-numbered 648. 642-647 were delivered in two batches of three in 1986-7. There should have been a further three Centenary cars, but Blackpool Transport Services did not proceed. Subsequently, there has been rebuilding of the cars, starting with 642 in 1999, improving its appearance with higher side roof and indicator boxes, new moquette seating and windows. When 641 was rebuilt in 2000, the advert box was removed and a standard pantograph tower fitted. Four more have been rebuilt by 2003, leaving 645 and 648 in original style.

Railcoach 204 was driven here from Bispham Depot and is sadly seen being stripped-down finally.
Author.

CARS SCRAPPED 1961 - 1965

DATE	CAR TYPE	PLACES	Nos.
1961 Feb 15	Marton Vambac 10.	Rigby Road.	1
1961 February	Standard 41.	Marton Depot.	1
1961 Feb 22	E.E Railcoach 206.	Bispham Depot.	1
1962 January	Maron Vambac 21.	Marton Depot.	1
1962 April 21	Pantographs 169,173,171.	Marton Depot.	3
1962 December	E.E Railcoach 203.	Rigby Road Works.	1
1962 February	Pantograph 172.	Rigby Road Works.	1
1963 Feb 26 to March 2	Marton Vambac 15,17,18,20. E.E Railcoaches 210,223. Pantograph 175.	All these cars were broken-up in Marton Depot by a contractor over a period of four weeks.	7
March 3 -9	Marton Vambac 12,13. Brush Vambac 303. E.E Railcoaches 200, 207.	Dates given week periods of scrapping. Depot cleared of scrap	5
March 9-23	Marton Vambac 14,16,19 Vambac Railcoach 208. E.E Railcoach 214.	and vacated by 8 April 1963.	5
1963 July	E.E Railcoaches 205, 219.	Rigby RoadWorks.	2
August 31	E.E Railcoach 202.	Thornton Gate Sidings.	1
September 19	E.E Railcoach 218.	Thornton Gate Sidings.	1
September 27	E.E Railcoach 201.	Thornton Gate Sidings.	1
October 30	E.E Railcoach 204.	Thornton Gate Sidings.	1
November 16	E.E Railcoach 215.	Thornton Gate Sidings.	1
1965 September	E.E Railcoaches 211,212,213,216,217.	Withdrawn from service in June 1965 and scrapped in Bispham Depot.	5
		TOTAL	38

CARS SCRAPPED 1968 - 2000

DATE		CAR TYPE	PLACES	Nos.
1968	March	Coronation 313.	Rigby Road Yard.	1
	April	Boats 229,231,232,234.	Blundell St. Depot.	4
		Brush Car 301.	Blundell St. Depot.	1
1969	February	Coronation 647,649,652.	Blundell St. Depot.	3
1970	May	Coronation 646,650,	Thornton Gate Sidings.	
	July	651,653,645,648.		6
1971	May	Coronation 642,643,	Rigby Road Yard.	
		644.658,659.		5
1972	August	Coronation 657,654,	Rigby Road Yard.	
	September	656,664.		4
1976	August	Coronation 661,655,	Rigby Road Yard.	
	September	662.		3
1980	January	Brush Car 629.	Blundell St. Depot.	1
1982	October	Trailer 688.	Blundell St. Depot.	
		Balloon 705.		2
1984	March	Brush Car 638.	Rigby Road Yard.	1
		OMO Cars 13.	Rigby Road Yard.	1
1987	March	OMO Cars 2,4,	Rigby Road Yard.	
	June	3.		3
1989	July	OMO Cars 6,9.	Rigby Road Yard.	2
1989		Trailer 689,690.	Bradford Carriage Shed.	2
1993	October	OMO Car 12.	Rigby Road Body Shop.	1
	December	OMO Car 1.	Rigby Road Body Shop.	1
2000	September	OMO Car 11.	Rigby Road Body Shop.	1
			TOTAL	42

Blundell Street depot in April 1968 as four Boats are broken-up, and it seems a great pity.

Author's Collection

(Above left) Tramnik One 732 in its original condition seen at North Pier in 1964. Built from Pantograph 168 in 1961, it is now owned by Lancastrian Transport Trust who gave its last run on 28 April 2002.

(Above Right) The Western Train 733-734 was built in 1962 from replacement railcoach 209 as the locomotive and Pantograph 174 as its carriage, seating completely 94 passengers. It has always been the most famous illuminated tram, however it was withdrawn in 1999. On Fleetwood Tram Sunday 2003, it was towed for display at Fleetwood Ferry, it may reappear again after rebuilding!

(Below) Hovertram 735 seen here passing tableaux in 1996. It was built from railcoach 222 in 1963 and carried 99 passengers with transverse seats and a side gangway on the upper deck. It ran in 2000, but is now stored for possible future restoration and it would be worth it!   Author

ILLUMINATED TRAMS

HMS Blackpool 736 - built in 1965 from Pantograph car 170 - seen here in Lord Street, Fleetwwod in 1985. It was withdrawn from use in 2000, because - like the other illuminated trams - 550 volts DC supplied the lighting directly. Its restoration commenced in 2003, and many radical changes are being made in the interests of public safety, with rewiring on 24 volts AC, and easier access for passengers by a larger nearside rear door, together with air-conditioning. Thus it can be used in service during the year, and not exclusively during the illuminations.

(Below) 736 is seen here during rebuilding, showing its new body-frame, doors and superstructure including the helicopter hangar and guided missiles. It will certainly look striking!   *Mike Airey*

The Works Cars

The sight of Whitegate Drive near Palatine Road with Railgrinder 1 (752), standing out amongst the traffic in 1953. It was built in 1928 with a Brill 21E truck from a Marton Box car, along with Railgrinder 2. The latter went to National Tramway Museum, and 752 is still here for rare use.

Author's Collection.

Works car for use on the PERMANENT WAY seen in Copse Road depot yard in 1962, showing Pantograph 170 for transporting the track-gang. It has just replaced 167, which had gone to Crich NTM in May 1962. The steeple-cab locomotive towed the rail-carrier bogies and here has the railway buffers to shunt railway wagons. Today it is at NTM for towing trams, without the buffers!

R. P. Fergusson.

TRAMCAR DEPOTS

Since there have been six tram depots in the past, today there is only one in Blackpool, which houses the fleet of 84 trams. All other depot buildings have disappeared, apart from Copse Road Depot at Fleetwood which is now a car sale-room but shows the headstones: B & F TRAMROAD & JUBILEE 1897.

BLUNDELL STREET, Princess Street, Blackpool

BUILT: 1884-85

CAPACITY: 45   TRACKS: 5

SERVICES WORKED: Before 1935 Promenade and Squires Gate services, during 1939-1944 operated the Marton route, from 1963 Promenade specials.

CARS: Range of cars until 1935; after 1963 illuminated cars, some Boats, Railcoaches and Standards - from closed Marton Depot.

HISTORY: Opened for ten conduit cars in 1885, extended in 1894 and 1896 for additional cars. In 1898 came the final extension to its full size, when the roof was raised for overhead wires. This was the main running shed until the opening of the new central depot in 1935, after which Blundell Street Depot became largely a store. In post-war years the inspection pits were filled in, and in 1956 the building was used as a bus garage. It was re-opened to trams in March 1963, to take the extra Promenade cars from Marton Depot, which closed at this time. A new entrance was made at the rear of the depot in July 1964, fronting on to Rigby Road with a four-track fan. Tracks 1, 2 & 5 could still be approached from the old entrance in Princess Street. Capacity was restricted by the presence of an ambulance station in the building. Following gale-damage to the central roof-frame, it was demolished from 4 November 1982, and the site became a car-park. With track will in place, it may qualify as a new historic transport museum!

The new entrance to the depot in 1964, with Brush works-car 624 towing the rail-carrier 628 passing in front of the Transport Office, about to make its first entry.   *Author.*

A fine view of Pantograph 170 standing in the yard of Copse Road depot in 1962.

R. P. Fergusson

FLEETWOOD (COPSE ROAD) DEPOT

BUILT: 1897

CAPACITY: 18 TRACKS: 6

SERVICES WORKED: Never a running shed, but also a store and workshop.

CARS: In Company days, crossbench cars and "box" saloons, in B.C.T. days works cars and the locomotive, used to store cars like famous Dreadnought 59.

HISTORY: Constructed in 1897 for the Blackpool and Fleetwood Tramroad Company and used from the first by service cars and then as a store. Passed to B.C.T. ownership in 1920 and was used prior to Second World War for breaking-up old trams. A line connected with the railway at the rear of the building and was used from 1925 to 1949 for shunting coal wagons, which were taken to Thornton Gate sidings with loads of coal. Since that time it was a permanent way store, until this was transferred to Thornton Gate sidings in January 1963. Today, it is a car showroom but the sub-station is still in the building and feeds the Fleetwood section.

FLEETWOOD (BOLD STREET) DEPOT

BUILT: 1899

CAPACITY: 4 TRACKS: 2

SERVICES WORKED: In Company days, North Station and Fleetwood.

CARS: Company "box" saloons.

HISTORY: Its construction was completed in January 1899, and the building was situated at the Fleetwood terminus of the Tramroad Company line. Used for the last two cars to Fleetwood at night, which became the first two cars from Fleetwood in the morning. Taken over by Blackpool Corporation in 1920 and never used as a depot. It was de-wired in 1924 when the new Ferry loop line was constructed, and rented to other concerns. In post-war years, it was used by the famous "Fisherman's Friend" and then demolished in 1973, for flats on site.

BISPHAM DEPOT: Red Bank Road, Bispham, Blackpool

BUILT: 1898

CAPACITY: 36 TRACKS: 6

SERVICES WORKED: Blackpool North Station and Fleetwood Ferry, with all short workings. Squires Gate and Bispham service shared with Rigby Road Depot from 1958 to 1961 in season. Starr Gate and Fleetwood in winter months.

CARS: All Company types, Pantographs cars 167-176, Brush cars 284-303, some E.E. series 1 railcoaches. Open Boat cars transferred from Marton Depot in March 1963. Always had an overhead line car - 4 (31) and later 3 (143).

HISTORY: Built in 1898 for Blackpool and Fleetwood Tramroad Company and extended to double its size in 1914. Operated cars on the North Station and Fleetwood service during its history, apart from 1935 to 1940 when it was a store. An electricity generating station was attached to the depot and became a sub-station with a mercury arc rectifier. Pantograph cars delivered new to this depot in 1928 and Brush cars in 1940, both types being associated with the shed. In 1950, the depot was closed when the track fan was relaid and the overhead altered to avoid "ducking" the trolleys at the doorway. During this period, Bispham cars operated from Blundell Street depot. The last service car to enter the shed was Brush car 290 on 27 October 1963, which was the last night for the operation of North Station and Fleetwood tram service. It remained as a store until 5 January 1966, when Coronation car 313 was towed away by Works car 5. It was sold and used as Alpic store until it was demolished in 1973 for Sainsburys supermarket. Its headstone is now on display at the National Tramway Museum, and the track fan was used at Heaton Park, and points stored for its future depot.

Bispham depot in 1963, engineering car 170 has just arrived and car 3 is inside. The original power-station can just be seen.   *Author*

MARTON DEPOT, Whitegate Drive, Blackpool

BUILT: 1901

CAPACITY: 50 TRACKS: 8

SERVICES WORKED: Prior to 1936, many town services operated from this depot, including Talbot Square and Layton. Talbot Square and Central Station via Marton, Talbot Square and South Pier or Royal Oak via Marton and Circular Tours. 1937-1962 Talbot Square and Royal Oak (extended to South Pier in Season until 1961), Circular Tours and Promenade specials.

CARS: Double-deck Standards, three Balloons for school-specials, Marton "Vambacs" 10-21, E.E. railcoaches, and twelve open "Boats".

HISTORY: Constructed in 1901 for the new Marton route to take 20 cars. Track fan curves were too tight to admit 4-wheel Box cars and alterations were made to fan and depot, which increased the capacity in the same year. Initially it was an important depot for all town services, but after 1936 abandonment of Layton and Central Drive sections, operated Marton services and Circular Tour, supplying extra cars for Promenade duties. Closed from 1939 to 1944 to trams, and used for aircraft construction by Vickers Aircraft Company. In May 1951, the building was decorated for the 50th anniversary of the Marton route. Closed for the winter from 1954 to 1959 as an economy measure. The last service cars were 48 from Royal Oak and 40 from Talbot Square on 28 October 1962, when Marton route was converted to bus operation. Power was finally switched-off on Monday, 11 March 1963, the last car left for Rigby Road being Standard 48. The front half of the depot was demolished for petrol station, rear half is commercial.

Standard 49 returns to Marton Depot after a day on the Promenade in August 1962. Notice the depot staff, one with a point-iron and the other with a trolley-pole. See the Blackpool coat-of-arms above.   *Author.*

This is the only depot today, seen here in the Seventies with a line-up of Balloons, OMOs, Frigate 736 and Boat 600. There are no doors, but you can imagine the original roller-blind doors.   *The Gazette*

RIGBY ROAD, Hopton Road, Blackpool

BUILT: 1935

CAPACITY: c.108 TRACKS: 18 originally

SERVICES WORKED: Until 1961:

Starr Gate and Fleetwood Ferry	Starr Gate and Thornton Gate
Squires Gate and Cabin	Pleasure Beach and Bispham
Fleetwood and Cleveleys	Cabin and Harrowside

Today:

Starr Gate and Fleetwood Ferry   Starr Gate and Cleveleys
Pleasure Beach & North Pier or Cabin or Bispham specials

CARS: Double-deck "Balloons", Coronations, Twin-cars, E.E. railcoaches. Today, the whole tram fleet represents many types, including Brush railcars from Bispham Depot, Boats and Standard 147 from Marton Depot, and historic cars: B & F Tramroad Box 40, Bolton 66, Stockport 5 and Sheffield 513.

HISTORY: This new car shed was built under the 5-year Plan of Modernisation and replaced Blundell Street and Bispham depots as running sheds. During the War, Marton Depot cars were housed at this depot, Bispham Depot was re-opened in 1940. Tracks 15-18 were enclosed by a partition to form an electrical Compound in September 1955. Modernisation of facilities at the depot 1962-63 included a mobile tram washing-plant, new aluminium folding doors to replace roller-blind doors, and a vacuum-cleaning plant. Track 18 was disused from 1982, when a storage plant for overhead line was built. A body-lift is at rear of track 11 to free bogies for servicing in the Works Fitting Shop. Today it is open-fronted and fully-lit and inspection pits run the full-length of tracks.

SOME WERE PRESERVED . . .

The National Tramway Museum in 1998, with Pantograph 167 and Toastrack 166. Crich Stand is towering over the scene, with the Emporium to the right.   *Author.*

Toastrack 166 showing PROMENADE at the town terminus of the national Tramway Museum in 1983, with the elegant scroll of the shelter.   *Author.*

Marton open-top 31 at Beamish North East Open Air Museum, and bound for TALBOT SQUARE. It was seen in Blackpool for the 1998 Centenary.   Author

Standard 48 bound for Lake Oswego on the Oregon Electric Railway from Portland, U.S.A. in June 2001.   Roy Bonn.

Standard 159 with London Transport HR2 1858 at the East Anglia Transport Museum, Carlton Colville, Lowestoft in July 2001. One is bound for LAYTON, and the other EMBANKMENT.
Bryan Grint.

LIST OF PRESERVED CARS

No.	TYPE	DATE LEFT	DESTINATION
144	Standard.	11 March 1955	Seashore Trolley Museum. Maine U.S.A.
167	Pantograph.	17 May 1962	NTM Crich, Derbyshire.
49	Standard.	13 December 1962	NTM Crich, Derbyshire.
4	Conduit Car.	18 March 1963	Museum British Transport, Clapham, London, & NTM.
2	B&F Crossbench.	17 September 1963	NTM Crich, Derbyshire.
40	Standard.	3 October 1963	NTM Crich, Derbyshire.
40	B&F Box-Car.	3 October 1963	NTM Crich, Derbyshire.
48	Standard.	24 August 1964	Oregon Electric Railway. Glenwood Oregon U.S.A.
59	Dreadnaught.	18 March 1965	NTM Crich, Derbyshire.
11	Marton Vambac.	9 September 1965	EATMS Carlton Colville, Lowestoft from 1969.
2	Grinder Car.	10 December 1965	NTM Crich, Derbyshire.
-	Electric Loco.	28 January 1966	NTM Crich, Derbyshire.
159	Standard.	18 April 1967	EATMS Carlton Colville.
147	Standard.	6 September 1967	Trolleyville, Ohio, U.S.A.
A TOTAL OF 14 TRAMCARS less Standard 147 returned in 2000!			

1. 144 Shipped from Liverpool to Boston U.S.A and arrived 28 March 1955
2. 48 Shipped from Hull to Portland via Panama Canal on " Sibonga"
3. 147 Shipped from Boston to Liverpool, arrived Blackpool 18 October 2000

No.	TYPE	DATE LEFT	DESTINATION
226	Boat Car	19 August 1971	Rio Vista,California U.S.A.
166	Toastrack	9 June 1972	NTM Crich, Derbyshire.
304	Coronation	16 July 1975	NTM Clay Cross Storage.
327	Coronation	19 August 1976	Lytham Railway Museum.
298	Brush Railcar	14 March 1977	NTM, Mode Wheel, Salford.
731	Blackpool Belle	18 March 1982	Glenwood Trolly Park, Oregon U.S.A.
31	Marton Open-Top	17 July 1984	N.E Open Air Museum. Beamish, Co. Durham.
228	Boat Car	19 February 1985	San Francisco MUNI, California, U.S.A.
5	OMO	2 June 2000	NTM, Clay Cross Store.
606	Boat Car	14 September 2000	Trolleyville & Cleveland Ohio, U.S.A.
753	Standard	13 April 2000	LTT Clifton Road Depot. Marton, Blackpool.
8	OMO	Stored in Depot	LTT.
732	Rocket	Stored in Depot	LTT.
A TOTAL OF 26 BLACKPOOL TRAMS ARE PRESERVED			

1. 31 returned to Blackpool for the Tramroad Centenary in 1998.
2. 304 returned to Blackpool 9 June 2002, restoring and filming for Salvage Squad.
3. Coronation 327 returned to LTT Clifton Road Depot, Marton on 13 April 2003